Simplifying Statistics for Graduate Students

Simplifying Statistics for Graduate Students

Making the Use of Data Simple and User-Friendly

Susan Rovezzi Carroll and David J. Carroll

ROWMAN & LITTLEFIELD
Lanham • Boulder • New York • London

Published by Rowman & Littlefield
An imprint of The Rowman & Littlefield Publishing Group, Inc.
4501 Forbes Boulevard, Suite 200, Lanham, Maryland 20706
www.rowman.com

86-90 Paul Street, London EC2A 4NE, United Kingdom

Copyright © 2023 by Susan Rovezzi Carroll and David J. Carroll

All rights reserved. No part of this book may be reproduced in any form or by any electronic or mechanical means, including information storage and retrieval systems, without written permission from the publisher, except by a reviewer who may quote passages in a review.

British Library Cataloguing in Publication Information Available

Library of Congress Cataloging-in-Publication Data Available

ISBN 9781475868388 (cloth) | ISBN 9781475868395 (pbk.) | ISBN 9781475868401 (ebook)

To all graduate students.

May this journey be one that you enjoy,
are proud of, and benefit from for many years.

Contents

	Introduction	ix
Chapter 1	Variables and How to Measure Them	1
Chapter 2	Intelligently Managing Your Data	11
Chapter 3	Graphing Techniques to Support Your Data	17
Chapter 4	Means, Medians, and Modes and When to Use Each	27
Chapter 5	Measuring Variability: An Important Role in Data	35
Chapter 6	Random Sampling and Other Useful Sampling Strategies	47
Chapter 7	Stating Hypotheses and Hypothesis Testing	55
Chapter 8	t-Test Procedures	63
Chapter 9	ANOVA Procedures	75
Chapter 10	Chi-Square Procedures	85
Chapter 11	Correlation Procedures	93
Chapter 12	Regression Procedures	103
Chapter 13	Practical Tips for Graduate Students	113
	About the Authors	121

Introduction

One of the greatest barriers to completing a graduate thesis or a doctoral dissertation is research that includes statistics. Oftentimes, the journey through graduate school is gratifying when the content courses in the chosen field of study are undertaken. Conversely, the courses in research methods and statistics are met with trepidation and anxiety. Many graduate students feel lost when it comes to dealing with data. Some students even quit at the end of their programs, which is why ABD (all but dissertation) applies to many PhDs.

This book is intended to help you move through the barriers that seem formidable *but are not*. This is not a statistics text and does not purport to be such. Rather, it is a way to introduce you to basic statistical concepts in a gentle, easy-to-comprehend manner so that you can become the success that you set out to be when you signed on to your academic journey.

Chapter 1 presents the concept of variables: What are they and how do you measure them? Knowing the differences in measurement scales, selecting the correct measurement scales for variables, and identifying which ones you use for different statistical procedures are significant steps in setting up data. This understanding is vital; the use of statistical procedures depends on this basic knowledge.

Next, chapter 2 discusses the steps needed to manage data sets. Oftentimes, the steps are bypassed allowing for errors and misinformation to emerge from data sets. Taking the time to develop frequency distributions and more importantly, examining them in detail, are some of the most valuable steps in data management.

Chapter 3 presents graphing techniques that are most beneficial to graduate students' research. Correctly choosing and then setting up graphs are discussed in this chapter along with some mistakes to avoid. Graphing can be an asset in the ability for graduate students to communicate their results in a simple, informative manner.

Chapter 4 begins the statistics presentation with descriptive statistics. The mean, median, and mode are used often every day. This chapter explains the three measures and when to use each one. Chapter 5 is a complement as it takes chapter 4 and explains why variability is critical as a partner to descriptive statistics. The benefit of understanding, and then using, the normal curve and percentiles is discussed in this chapter.

Chapter 6 shows graduate students the different sampling strategies. It explains the process of random sampling and also includes several other sampling strategies that might be of use in different situations. Especially important is the presentation of nonrandom sampling options, which may be more practical for graduate student research.

Chapter 7 reviews hypothesis testing as a prerequisite to running statistical analyses. It is imperative to state the research question and corresponding null hypothesis that statistics will be used to test. Type I and Type II errors, along with the Bonferroni correction, are examined.

Chapters 8 and 9 begin the introduction of inferential statistics. T-tests and ANOVA (analysis of variance) procedures are examined in a straightforward manner so that graduate students can confidently execute them. These parametric statistics have application in many graduate research designs where two or more groups are compared on some measure.

In chapter 10 the nonparametric statistic chi-square analysis is presented. Because this procedure examines categorical variables such as demographics, its usage to graduate students is immense.

Correlation and multiple regression are presented in chapters 11 and 12. Correlation is a descriptive statistic that tests relationships among variables. This allows graduate students to avoid speculating about what is and is not related. The correlation coefficients do the work. Multiple regression is a complex, multivariate procedure presented in a basic and uncomplicated manner. This statistic has many applications but may require external expertise to help execute it.

Chapter 13 gives graduate students advice on determining their research topic, using library references, selecting a research design, and writing up results from their data. Strategies to do this with finesse, accuracy, and honesty are offered to help graduate students make the most of their data.

Expertise with data is expected of graduate students. It is part of the reason you are earning an advanced degree. *Simplifying Statistics for Graduate Students: Making the Use of Data Simple and User-Friendly* is an antidote for the research and statistics blues. It can provide graduate students with the confidence they need when signing on to the research methods and statistics courses required in their programs. Graduate students should enjoy the journey and this book can help.

CHAPTER ONE

Variables and How to Measure Them

Few of us eagerly anticipate taking a research or statistics course. That included me in my own graduate program. Many times, there is a knowledge gap between high school mathematics and the quantitative courses of graduate study. For some, math was a subject in high school taken primarily as a college application requirement. For others, the image of statistics was and remains formula-driven, and thus intricately complex and intimidating. Some of those brave souls who have taken a statistics course most likely had their preconceptions confirmed by a professor who taught the subject from a computational perspective.

Consequently, many graduate students and new faculty are wary of pursuing research based on data. This is unfortunate; it can be so exciting! This book is not a statistics text. It is a book for those who want to use data for their thesis, dissertation, or faculty research with a sense of confidence.

Look at the data set in textbox 1.1 that represents pre- and posttest values for only twenty-eight subjects. It can make your head spin. What can you tell from "eyeballing" the data set?

- Are most subjects performing well or performing poorly?
- What is the typical performance score in the data?
- Are subjects making gains–if so, to what degree?
- Are segments of subjects (by gender, age, ethnicity) performing differently?
- How does performance compare with peers?

Textbox 1.1. Pre- and Postdata Set for 28 Subjects

```
001   2221222132111211201021202011102011111210122011221011
002   1311113131112300301113113111101333121321111101110110
003   32213221322122102020211030    212020012002103120002011
004   3330333123300320002032203213030012002101030000300031
005   221122132321121120112211121    2311211122021    231201121111
006   1221122111111211211121212111111011110211111001211111
007   2221222123311212020321131301131200210121    1212000310211
008   22112211122102111011222120121121012112113110102111122
009   3331332123210220310021303021302031300330303000320030
010   3330333033200320303133103022302000200310201000220021
011   321032213221021020103220201021200110011111011111111
012   333133203321032030200323130    3330311110032    031300122012
013   333032313220031031303130302    331100120021    031200122013
014   1201221102211202102011023013301103100310012001120111
015   22212221222002102131301020113120033101003130012200111
016   1310321232100101300031103013321103110110321001310101
017   22012210320212012111231231101012100131011110302003101
018   22012210320212012111231231101012100131011110302003101
019   23302320233123133021212030112021123012103030102100111
020   3200120133101100201021020010011003010100313001010131
021   2221332033210311212032202022103001211301313002330030
022   2320322112310320212131102011212002110212130001100312
023   332131221331010030013000211121210031021032103133230002
024   3320232022300320301032303000    203030001002303020001100210
025   121122212231121131211121111212211111121221210111121111
026   22202320132013301111212011    2120101110111    0311001110131
027   23312230323013023021122211    2310212210211    0122011122210
028   23312221122012102011222120    2120210121121    1112001221121
```

Most of us cannot answer these questions by reviewing a set of data. Even the small set of 28 pre- and postvalues displayed in textbox 1.1 is incomprehensible. Our human minds are limited in their capacity to absorb a set of numbers, retain them, process them, and then make sense of them.

Statistics is an area of math that seeks to make order out of a diverse collection of facts. With a single number, statistics can summarize the properties of large groups of numbers. They help us to obtain an understanding of our data. Statistical techniques summarize data, making complex masses of numbers simple. By using them, we are able to crunch large sets of numbers into usable and actionable information.

Basically, statistics should be thought of as numbers that summarize the properties of large groups of numbers. If you have been given a massive assortment of data and have no hope of understanding them, although you have looked at them for hours, use statistics. Life will become less complicated.

General Classifications of Data: Quantitative and Qualitative

Statistics involves collecting information called data, analyzing it, and making meaningful decisions based on the data. Collected data, which represent observations or measurements of something of interest, can be classified into two general types: qualitative and quantitative.

- The term *qualitative data* refers to observations that are descriptive. These data represent categories. This might include demographic data such as gender, ethnicity/race, town of residency, education, household composition, and others.
- The term *quantitative data* represent various observations or measurements that are numerical such as academic grades, blood pressure readings, customer satisfaction ratings, attendance, and others.

The Essential Component in Data: Variables

Data are derived from characteristics about individuals, objects, or events. These characteristics are called *variables*. Anything that varies and can be measured is called a variable. Variables can be quantitative or qualitative. We attach numbers to our variables in an effort to measure them and apply statistics to them.

Variables that are qualitative are called *categorical* variables. They have different categories, and each category takes on a whole number or integer to represent it. For example, *school type* would be a categorical variable. For some school systems it might have three categories:

1 = Elementary (Kindergarten through fifth grade)
2 = Middle (sixth through eighth grades)
3 = Secondary (ninth through twelfth grades)

Variables that are quantitative are classified as either *discrete* or *continuous*. If they are discrete, they can take on only whole numbers or integers. For example, discrete variables might include number of children in the home, total number of hospital admissions, SAT scores, number of DUIs, or monthly deaths from COVID-19. These are represented by whole numbers. If they are continuous variables, they can take on fractions or decimals. Body weight, credit card balance, body temperature, height, or race time are examples of continuous variables, where race time in the 100-meter dash might be 13.2 seconds. See table 1.1 for a classification of variables.

Table 1.1. Classification Chart for Data and Variables

Qualitative Data	Categorical Variables	Whole Numbers Only	Residential Locations Urban (1) Rural (2) Suburban (3)
Quantitative Data	Discrete Variables	Whole Numbers Only	Hospital Readmissions 3, 5, 8
	Continuous Variables	Fractions and Decimals	Grade Point Average 3.29

All variables are measurable, or they would not be called variables. We have to assign numbers to all of our variables in order to apply statistics to them. In order to do this, we have to understand the scales of measurement. This is essential. Unfortunately, it is an area that is largely misunderstood. If measurement scales are used incorrectly, the wrong statistical technique will be applied to the data. This will yield erroneous information.

Four Measurement Scales

Whatever exists, exists in some amount and can be measured. *Measurement* involves quantifying people, objects, or events on their characteristics. When we collect information about people, objects, and events, we must turn that information into numbers so that we can measure it and make deductions about what we find out. We must express it in numbers not just descriptive phrases.

Because measurement involves quantifying people, objects, or events on their characteristics, you must assign numbers to variables. There are four scales of measurement used to assign numbers to variables. Each is differentiated according to their degree of precision. For example, a pediatrician might measure a child's general health by level of physical activity, nutritional practices, and weight. The latter is the most precise measure although all three can provide information about the same variable—health.

Nominal Measurement Scales

The first measurement scale in the hierarchy is the *nominal* scale. The term "nominal" means to name. The properties of nominal scales are:

- Data categories are mutually exclusive.
- Data categories have no logical order.

Observations are simply classified into categories and assigned a number with no relationship existing between or among the categories. It classifies without ordering. The variable Home Loan Application can be nominally scaled with a number of either 1 (complete) or 0 (incomplete) categories. Another example is the variable of Workshop Attendance; it would have nominal scaling—present (1) or absent (0).

The numeric values could be any combination. Three options for nominal coding of the same variable, such as *Residential Location*, are presented in table 1.2.

Table 1.2. Three Nominal Scale Options for the Variable *Residential Location*

Option One		Option Two		Option Three	
Variable	Numbers Assigned	Variable	Numbers Assigned	Variable	Numbers Assigned
Rural	1	Rural	2	Rural	3
Urban	2	Urban	3	Urban	2
Suburban	3	Suburban	1	Suburban	1

There is no logical ordering of the categories. Numbers are assigned to the categories, but no quantitative meaning is assigned to the numbers. The numbers mean absolutely *nothing*. We are simply using the numbers to classify people, objects, and events. The numbers we assign to those categories have no ordering, no ranking, no "higher than," no "lower than," no "more of," or no "less than" associated with them. They are what their name suggests—nominal, a name to identify. The numbers we assign to our variables in their categories are not quantifiable except to count them up. The total number of males we have will be how many we add up with the value we have assigned to it. This is important to note when you are calculating statistics.

There are two basic requirements for nominal measurement:

1. All members of one category must be assigned the same numeral.
2. No two categories are assigned the same numeral.

Some nominally scaled variables have only two categories. These are called *dichotomous* variables. This means that only two numbers can be assigned to each of the categories, respectively. Some examples of dichotomous variables may include primary language spoken at home (English/Spanish), parent (father/mother), staff (supervisor/trainee), student (special education/ general education), loan applicant (accepted/rejected), patient (inpatient/ outpatient), and many others. You may use two numbers (such as 1 and 2 *or* 0 and 100 *or* 200 and 300) as the nominal scaling applied to each category.

Nominal scaling is ideal to categorize schools. The type of school the child attends might be categorized as Elementary (1), Middle (2), and Secondary (3). Or, if we have five elementary schools, we could nominally scale all seven of the schools that the children in a town attend as in table 1.3.

Table 1.3. Nominal Scale for a School System with Seven Schools (Five Elementary)

Schools in the School System	Number Assigned
Peachtree Elementary School	1
Riverside Elementary School	2
Justin Elementary School	3
Harris Elementary School	4
Connor Elementary School	5
Maples Middle School	6
Maples High School	7

Being able to nominally scale our variables this way allows us to drill down our data or inspect our data much more thoroughly.

One pitfall threatens. Many individuals get confused about what the actual variable is and what are the respective categories. Sometimes, you might think the *variable* is female instead of gender with categories. This differentiation is very important, especially when you are investigating statistical differences with independent and dependent variables, which will be discussed later in the book. Ask yourself: What variable are the individual categories representing? The answer should be the variable itself and not its categories.

Ordinal Measurement Scales

The second type of scaling in the measurement hierarchy is called *ordinal*, where there is relative ranking and ordering of an attribute in different categories. There is "more than" and "less than," "higher than" and 'lower than," "least of" and "most of." There is a qualitative relationship among numbers in the ordinal scale. Unlike nominal scaling, the numbers in ordinal scales have meaning. Ordinal scales give more information and more precise data than nominal scales do. Here are three examples of ordinal-scaled variables:

Variable: Frequency
Never (1)
Rarely (2)
Sometimes (3)
Frequently (4)
Always (5)

Variable: Satisfaction
Dissatisfied (1)
Satisfied (2)
Very Satisfied (3)

Variable: Attainment
Below Expectations (1)
Meets Expectations (2)
Exceeds Expectations (3)

The properties of ordinal scales are:

- Data categories are mutually exclusive.
- Data categories have some logical order.
- Data categories are scaled according to the amount of a particular characteristic they possess.

One of the most common uses of ordinal scaling is with ratings, preferences, rankings, goal attainment, satisfaction, degrees of quality, and agreement levels—typical of the Likert scale found on questionnaires. Here is an example of ordinal scaling using a rubric to measure student performance:

Beginning (1)
Developing (2)
Proficient (3)
Advanced (4)

As a note, it is helpful to assign your numbers in ordinal scaling in ways that make sense. A rating of "excellent" on a 5-point rating scale can have a value of 5 or a value of 1. It is relatively arbitrary. However, it makes more conceptual sense that a low rating with a value of 1 should be assigned to a low rating—"poor," whereas a high rating (5) should be assigned to a high rating—"excellent." After you tabulate your data, it is easier to interpret what you have found out if you assign your ordinal numbers in gradations that make sense.

Another example of ordinal scaling that is used often is applied to agreement statements. There are five responses that could be assigned ordinal values. Again, it makes more conceptual sense to assign the value "1" to the least amount of agreement—Strongly Disagree and vice versa. Higher levels of agreement should be reflected in the values assigned—5 = Strongly Agree. Again, this is arbitrary.

Strongly Disagree (1)
Disagree (2)
Undecided/Uncertain (3)
Agree (4)
Strongly Agree (5)

Interval and Ratio Measurement Scales

There are two metric scales of measurement: interval and ratio scales. Because of their metric nature, these two measurement scales afford the most precise data. With both there are equal intervals or units between any two consecutive numbers. For interval and ratio scales, the distance between numbers 2 and 3 and between 4 and 5 are exactly the same. This is different from ordinal scales where we cannot claim for certain that the distance between good (3) and fair (2) is exactly the same as between poor (1) and fair (2). We assign numbers in ordinal scales, but the distance is not in exact units. With interval and ratio scales, there is the ordering that is found in ordinal scales, but now we have exact units of measurement.

The only difference between interval and ratio scales is the role of zero (0). In interval scales zero is artificial rather than real. For ratio scales, the role of zero is real; there is the absence of that variable being measured.

With these two scales we can compute high-level, sophisticated statistics called parametric statistics (which will be discussed later in the book).

The properties of interval scales are:

- Data categories are mutually exclusive.
- Data categories have a definite logical order.

- Data categories are scaled according to the amount of a particular characteristic they possess.
- Equal differences in the characteristics are represented by equal differences in the numbers assigned to the categories.
- The point zero (0) is just another point on the scale.

Interval scaling is used often in graduate student research. When we measure leadership, personality, aptitude, interests, attitudes, achievement, and other variables, it is likely that they are measured on interval scaling.

Ratio scaling is similar to interval scaling in terms of equivalent values between numbers. The only difference is that in ratio scales a zero (0) means something important. It means the absence of whatever the scale is measuring. This type of scaling is encountered more commonly in the physical sciences where there can really be "none"—weight, time, height, calories, or wherever zero is real, not artificially created. If you are measuring the level of pain in postsurgical patients (where none is possible), you would be using ratio scaling.

The properties of ratio scales are:

- Data categories are mutually exclusive.
- Data categories have a definite logical order.
- Data categories are scaled according to the amount of a particular characteristic they possess.
- Equal differences in the characteristics are represented by equal differences in the numbers assigned to the categories.
- The point zero (0) reflects absence of the characteristic.

Chapter Summary

As a summary of the four measurement scales, they can be remembered by the following characteristics:

- *Nominal*: numbers are assigned without order and meaning.
- *Ordinal*: numbers are assigned with order but without equal intervals between them.
- *Interval*: numbers are assigned with order and equal units.
- *Ratio*: numbers are assigned with order, equal units, and a true zero point.

When setting up data, graduate students must know the information covered in this first chapter. It is the foundation of being data literate. Knowing what the differences are in measurement scales, selecting the correct measurement scales for variables, and identifying which ones to use for different statistical procedures are significant steps in setting up data. This understanding is vital; the use of statistical procedures depends on this basic knowledge.

CHAPTER TWO

Intelligently Managing Your Data

Often, when we look at a set of data, it is basically a blur of numbers. This is easily addressed by displaying data with a method to the madness. There are several steps that graduate students should follow when they are working with data sets.

The first step is simply organizing your data. Many graduate students skip this step because it is elementary and seems too simple to be useful. It is advised that you take the time to organize your data. Doing this will help you to understand your data and make preliminary conclusions. Equally important, you will be familiarized with the data to the point where oversights can be uncovered, avoiding embarassment to you and minimizing the value of your work.

Frequency Distributions

One of the most useful expenditures of time is to produce a *frequency distribution* for each of the variables in your data set. This is a systematic arrangement of numeric values from the highest to the lowest—with a count of the number of times each value was obtained. It is a procedure for organizing and summarizing data into a meaningful representation. It does not tell you everything about your data, but it provides a beginning and convenient way of grouping data so that meaningful patterns can be found. Statistical packages like SPSS can do this for you, but here is how you do it if you did it yourself.

The first step in developing a frequency distribution is to put all your values for one variable in order from the lowest value to the highest value in a column format. Then, use slash marks or *tally* marks beside every value in your column—each and every time it occurs. Some values may occur only once, and some may occur more often. This is why tallies are helpful. Lastly, count up the tally marks and place a real number beside them that shows the frequency that each value occurred in your distribution. This information in chart form can make sense of a set of numbers that appears to be a jumble at first glance.

There are symbols that are typically used. When we set up our frequency distributions, the lowercase letter "x" indicates our values, and the lowercase letter "f" indicates the frequency of occurrence. For example, let's say your website click-through data look like the data set shown in table 2.1.

Table 2.1. Data Set for Daily Website Clicks for 50 Days

Week	Monday	Tuesday	Wednesday	Thursday	Friday
1	699	459	450	450	445
2	420	420	420	420	420
3	430	420	445	435	467
4	420	320	420	320	420
5	689	445	479	450	467
6	435	430	430	430	420
7	420	467	467	450	435
8	320	320	320	320	420
9	430	445	430	435	467
10	420	420	320	420	467

The lowest number of clicks is 320 and the highest is 699. The frequency distribution orders the 50-day click rates from lowest to highest and then tally marks are placed to show the frequency each was obtained. Percentages (the relative frequencies) are calculated to provide even more information to you. Finally, cumulative frequencies and cumulative percentages are added to complete the picture (review table 2.2).

From this frequency distribution, you can draw some important conclusions:

- The most frequently occurring click rate was 420—the most typical for 30% of the days.
- More than half (56%) of the click rates were 430 or lower.

Table 2.2. **Frequency Distribution for Daily Website Clicks (N = 50 days)**

Clicks	Tallies	Frequency (f)	Relative Frequency	Cumulative Frequency	Cumulative Frequency
320	///////	7	14%	7	14%
420	///////////////	15	30%	22	44%
430	//////	6	12%	28	56%
435	////	4	8%	32	64%
445	////	4	8%	36	72%
450	////	4	8%	40	80%
459	/	1	2%	41	82%
467	//////	6	12%	47	94%
479	/	1	2%	48	96%
689	/	1	2%	49	98%
699	/	1	2%	50	100%

- There is a broad range of click rates from highest (699) to lowest (320).
- Two click rates (699 and 689) were very different from the other rates—*outliers*.

Class Intervals

Let's say that you have twice as many days in your sample: 100 instead of 50. You might use a shorthand called *class intervals*. The number of classifications of data (classes) can be reduced by combining several of the actual clicks into an interval or band of values. You are essentially consolidating the data points into bundles to make them more manageable and comprehensible.

A good rule of thumb is to have between 10 to 20 class intervals, altogether. This is particularly true if you intend to graph your frequency distribution data into a frequency polygon or histogram, which will be discussed in the next chapter. Ten to 20 class intervals will summarize your data without distorting the shape of your graph. Too few intervals compress the data and thus conceal meaningful changes in the shape of your graph. Too many intervals stretch out the data, so they are not summarized enough for a clear visualization.

There are two general rules for using class intervals:

- The class interval should be of such size that between 10 and 20 intervals will cover the total range of values. This provides for a manageable number of intervals without losing the general shape of the distribution.
- Whenever possible, the width of the class interval should be an odd rather than an even number. Under this rule, the midpoint of the

interval will be a whole number rather than a fraction. This will become important when you graph your data.

How to Construct a Frequency Distribution Using Class Intervals

1. First, determine the range in your frequency distribution from your highest value to your lowest value. For the point of illustration, let's say we have a low of 320 and a high of 767. The difference or range is (767 − 320) = 447.
2. Divide the range by either 10 or 20 to get the number of intervals that makes the most sense and is most manageable. For 10, you would divide 447 by 10, and it would yield 45, as the class interval. For 20, you would divide 447 by 20 and get 22, as the class interval. For the sake of illustration, we choose 10; so, our class interval is 45.
3. Begin your intervals a little below your lowest value; in our data it is 320. With 45-point increments, our first-class interval is 300–344.
4. Once you set up your class intervals, then you proceed the same way you did with the frequency distribution in Table 2.2. Use tallies for the interval in which your values fall. A tally would include a click rate of 396 in the interval of 391–436.

Table 2.3 displays what our frequency distribution *with class intervals* would look like.

Table 2.3. Frequency Distribution of Daily Website Clicks *with Class Intervals* (N = 100 days)

Class Intervals of 45	Tallies	Frequency (f)	Relative Frequency	Cumulative Frequency	Cumulative Frequency
300–344	/	1	1%	1	1%
345–390	//////	6	6%	7	7%
391–436	/////////////////////////	25	25%	32	32%
437–482	putting didn't work—18 tallies	18	18%	50	50%
483–528	///////////	11	11%	61	61%
529–574	////////////	12	12%	73	73%
575–620	/////////	9	9%	82	82%
621–666	//////	6	6%	88	88%
667–712	//////	6	6%	94	94%
713–758	/////	5	5%	99	99%
759–804	/	1	1%	100	100%

As you can see, using class intervals to compose a frequency distribution makes it easy to analyze as well as to present your data. Again, important conclusions can be drawn:

- Most of the click rates were low.
- The most frequently occurring click rates were between 391 and 436.
- There is a broad range of click rates from below 345 to over 758.
- There were a few extremely high and extremely low click rates.

As a note, using class intervals is less cumbersome when your data are continuous and have a wide range of values. Think about the variable of *age* and the adults in your community if you were conducting a survey of city residents. Listing all possible ages might begin at 18 and go beyond 100 or more years! Doing a tally of each and every age would require a lot of paper, never mind time. This is a case when categorizing your variable into class intervals is a good idea. You might use intervals of five years in this case so those class intervals would look like this. (There would be less than 20 intervals for adult ages.)

Class Intervals for Age for City Residents

18–22
23–27
28–32
33–37
38–42
43–47
48–52
53–57
58–62
63–67
68–72 and so forth.

On the other hand, there are times when using class intervals shortchanges the picture; you lose valuable data. Think about the variable "*years that nurses have been employed by your hospital.*" If you used class intervals, you would lose key information. A nurse who is brand-new, one who has been with you for only one year, and one who has been on staff for three years may be very different from each other. If you collapsed the "years employed" into intervals of five years as shown with the age data, you would lose important insights. Much of this is common sense. What is the information you want to uncover with your data?

Why Frequency Distributions Are Helpful

Whenever you compile a set of data, it is highly recommended that you first set up (or run-on SPSS) a frequency distribution and study it. This is a strong recommendation. *Do not skip this step.* Knowing your data thoroughly is critical before you begin to dig deeper. Besides developing an expertise with your data set, there are several practical aspects to the development of frequency distributions:

- You can identify atypical or odd values like that in table 2.2 (689 and 699). You have to be able to identify *outliers* before you can determine what you should do with them. And it is important to decide whether to keep or discard *outliers*. They can skew your results!
- You can compare the spread the values, visually. If you set up two frequency distributions representing two segments of your data (such as Weeks 1–5 and Weeks 6–10), you might be able to infer why the click rates varied.
- By indicating the frequency that each value occurred in the distribution, this information could help you to make decisions about statistical analyses you will execute later. This is particularly true with categorical variables. For example, if you wanted to categorize click rates into high, moderate, and low, you might look at the percentages to classify them.
- Finally, the frequency distribution may reveal data entry errors that you typed in accidentally. If you had a click rate of 9 or 9999 that showed up in your frequency distribution, you would know that that was an error. You would be able to make your correction and not run the data blindly, compromising the purity of your data set. This happens often when frequency distributions are not run on all the data before the statistical analyses are executed. Take the time to do the basic work before you plunge into the analytics.

Chapter Summary

The process of becoming an expert with your data takes work. Setting up the frequency distribution for your data set, graphing it, and then interpreting what it conveys, are often-skipped steps in data management. The time it takes to do the "grunt" work as a preliminary step is a meaningful investment of time. There are advantages to be gained in many areas. You will be able to reduce errors, make wise decisions about statistical techniques, and ultimately provide a better foundation for interpreting your results. Take the time to know your data set. It will be well worth the hours spent. Don't shortchange yourself and compromise your research quality.

CHAPTER THREE

Graphing Techniques to Support Your Data

The Shapes of Graphs from Distributions

The frequency distribution is an excellent tool for displaying and inspecting your dissertation or thesis data. Yet it does not convey the information as quickly or as impressively as graphs do. Graphs allow us to see the shape of a distribution. They are designed to help obtain an intuitive feeling for the data at a glance. The message should be readily apparent.

An effective graph is simple and clean. It should not attempt to present so much information that it is difficult to comprehend the message. It should be complete within itself and require little if any explanation in the narrative.

Benefits of Using Graphs

Graphs are most beneficial because they can provide you with a summary data sheet as well as an opportunity to eyeball data. By looking at the *shape of the curve* (the hump) in your graph you can make some general conclusions quickly about the values in your data set. The illustrations in figures 3.1 through 3.5 will help in interpreting shapes.

- If the curve has a hump in the middle, its symmetry means that you have most values in the middle of the range—few high and few low. (Normal curve, as in figure 3.1.)

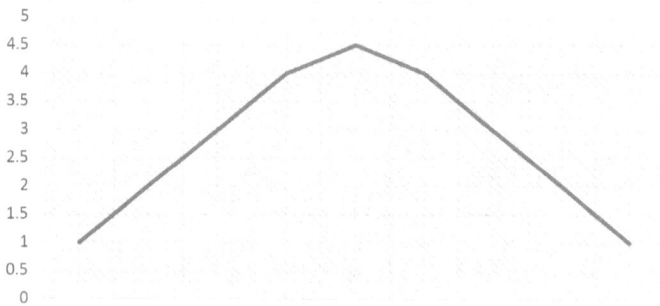

Most values are in the middle with few high and few low values.

Figure 3.1. Normal Curve. *Source: Author developed*

- If the hump of the curve is inclined toward the left, you have more low values in your data set. The tail or end of this type of curve indicates atypical or odd values in your data. In this case, there was a minority of high values. (Positively skewed, as in figure 3.2.)

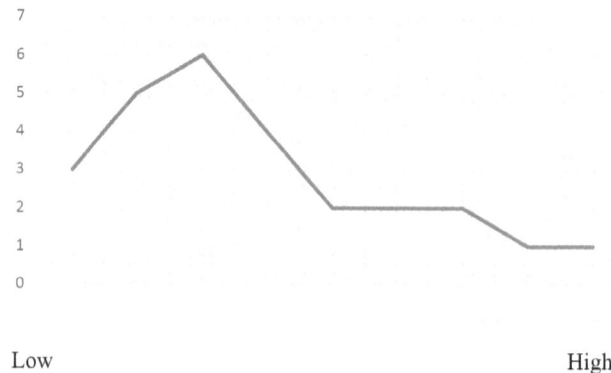

Mostly low values in frequency distribution and few high values.

Figure 3.2. Positively Skewed Curve. *Source: Author developed*

- If the hump of the curve is to the right, you have more high values in your data set. The tail or end of this type of curve indicates atypical or odd values in your data. In this case, there was a minority of low values. (Negatively skewed, as in figure 3.3.)

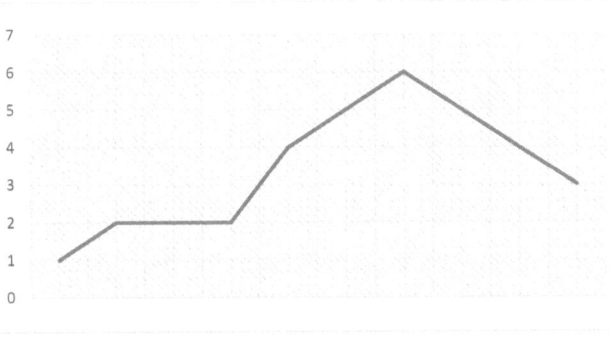

Mostly high values in frequency distribution and few low values.

Figure 3.3. Negatively Skewed Curve. *Source: Author developed*

- If the hump of the curve is flat, you have values that are spread out a great deal. Values are all over the map. (Platykurtic as in figure 3.4.)

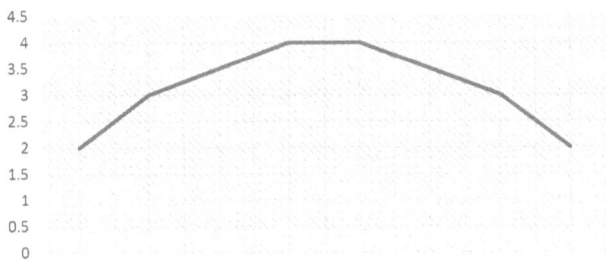

Values are spread out and there is no common performance.

Figure 3.4. Platykurtic Curve. *Source: Author developed*

- If the hump of the curve is peaked, your values are very, very similar. There is not much difference among values. (Leptokurtic as in figure 3.5.)

20 ~ Chapter Three

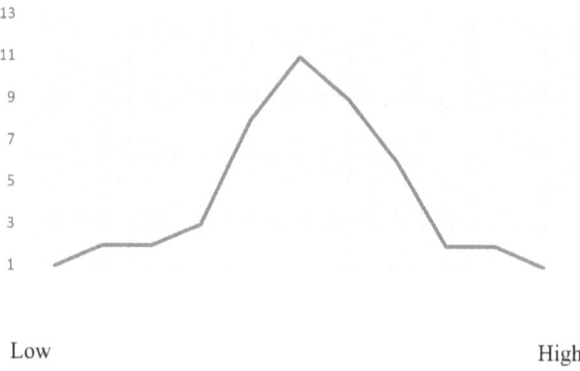

Values are very similar with few differences among values.

Figure 3.5. Leptokurtic Curve. Source: Author developed

The discussion about the shapes of graphs will have more meaning in subsequent chapters.

Types of Graphs

Frequency Polygons

To construct a graph from a set of data, we start with the frequency distribution. A frequency distribution can be graphed into a *frequency polygon*. This is how you convert a frequency distribution into a frequency polygon.

Draw a vertical side or *ordinate* axis of your graph. This is called the Y axis. On the Y axis it is an accepted practice for the frequencies to be plotted. The horizontal axis, called the *abscissa*, is used to plot the variable that you are displaying data for. The horizontal axis is the X axis. As a rule of thumb for good visual presentation, the vertical axis should be roughly two-thirds the length of the horizontal axis.

Connect the points with a dot that intersects the values on the abscissa axis to the frequencies on the ordinate axis. If class intervals are used, connect the midpoint of the interval on the horizontal axis with the frequency on the vertical axis. (This is why it is helpful to use odd numbers for the span of your class interval. The midpoint is easy to identify.) As a note, if the range in frequencies is large, you may want to start the vertical axis with a value that is not zero (0).

Plotting the data this way allows the graph to take on a shape. When you look at that shape, you can make a conclusion about the data from the frequency distribution. When there are a lot of data from many values, the frequency polygon looks like a smooth curve. When there are fewer values, it is jagged. Either way, the picture tells a story. The graph is a picture that gives us an immediate message about our data. We look at it and we can infer something about our data.

For our daily website click graph with class intervals, the simple message is that there are many low values in this distribution, and it is a positively skewed curve (see figure 3.6).

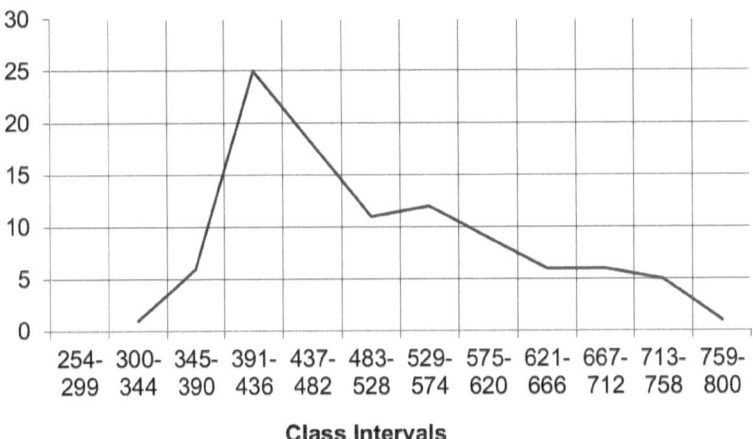

Figure 3.6. Frequency Polygon of Website Clicks. *Source: Author developed*

Bar Graph

A *bar graph* is a very convenient graphing device that is particularly useful for displaying nominal data such as gender, ethnicity, and other categorical variables. The various categories are located along the horizontal axis. The frequency or count, as always, is on the vertical axis. The height of each bar is equal to the frequency for that category. This is very helpful for viewing the differences in the data for individual groups on some variable.

If your dissertation or thesis were presenting demographics on households with and without children, and there were 200 households in your sample, the results in the bar graph would be obvious. Even without the actual numbers inside the bars, the two columns of the bar graph show that twice as many respondents did not have children as compared with those who did. Please refer to figure 3.7.

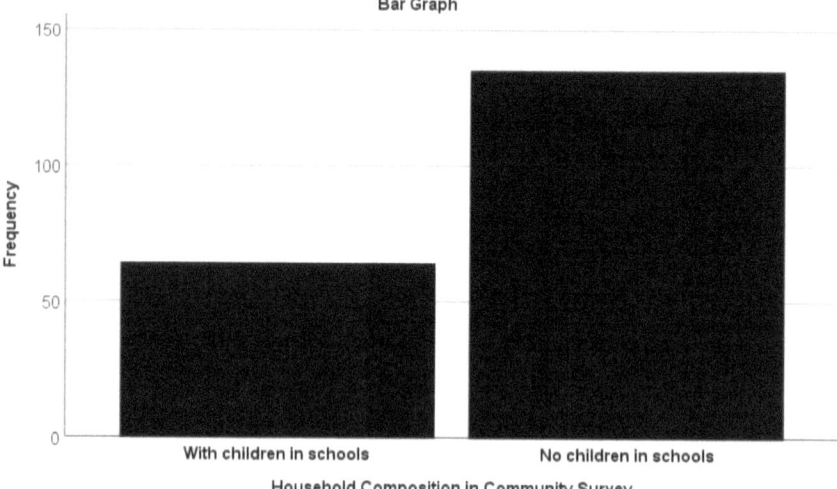

Figure 3.7. Bar Graph of Household Composition. *Source: Author developed*

Histograms

A *histogram* is another pictorial representation of a frequency distribution. While bar graphs are useful for nominal-scaled, categorical variables, the histogram is preferred if there is a quantitative variable where categories have gradations such as age or income. A general rule in laying out the histogram is to make the height of the vertical axis equal to approximately two-thirds the length of the horizontal axis. Otherwise, the histogram may appear to be out of proportion.

A vertical bar is constructed above each respective category equal in height to its frequency count. All the rectangles have equal width. This is a very common way to display data. Figure 3.8 displays what a histogram would look like if you were reporting age segments. The age differences in the respondents can immediately be seen. There are many respondents who were older.

The Difference Between a Histogram and Bar Graph

One difference between a histogram and a bar graph is that with the histogram the bars are placed next to each other to show continuity between the gradations; when one interval begins, the other one ends. The data bars in *histograms* have values attached to them and are continuous, such as with the variable of age segments in figure 3.8. However, because the data are nominal scaled in *bar graphs*, and not related to each other, the bars must not be connected so any implication of continuity is prevented. This is illustrated in figure 3.7.

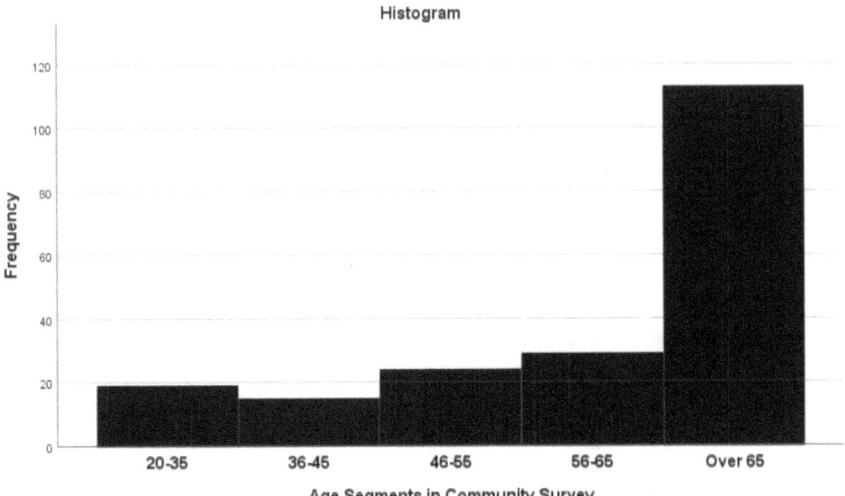

Figure 3.8. **Histogram of Age Segements.** *Source: Author developed*

Pictographs

A *pictograph* uses pictures or symbols in place of numbers. Figure 3.9 portrays a pictograph of the number of books read by a fourth-grade class during the holiday vacation week. It uses a book icon, representing five books read for each day Monday through Friday.

Days of Week				
Monday	📖			
Tuesday	📖			
Wednesday	📖	📖		
Thursday	📖	📖		
Friday	📖	📖	📖	📖

📖 = 5 books read by 4th Grade class

Figure 3.9. Pictograph of Books Read by 4th Graders. *Source: Author developed*

Pie Charts

Another method to display data is by using a *pie chart*. This graph is very easy to generate and is user-friendly. It shows the categories of a variable by dividing up "the pie." Use 100% of the area in the circle and divide it up proportionally to the categories of interest. Figures 3.10 and 3.11 display pie charts that reflect the same data on *Household Composition* and *Age Segments* for respondents, as depicted on the histogram and bar graph, previously shown.

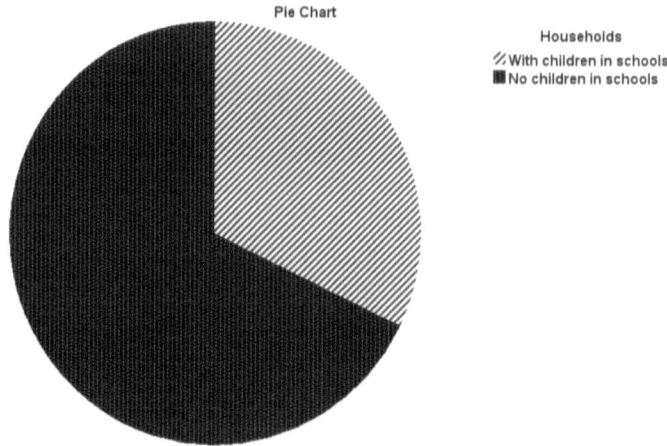

Figure 3.10. Pie Chart of Household Composition. *Source: Author developed*

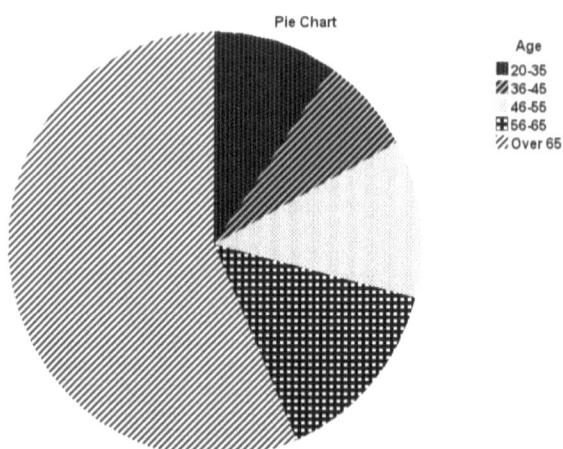

Figure 3.11. Pie Chart of Age Segments. *Source: Author developed*

Advice for Developing Graphs

Graphing is an excellent way to demonstrate your data to the untrained eye. There are two recommendations to observe when constructing your graphs.

1. A graph is a picture. So the message should be readily apparent. Keeping it simple is a good practice to follow when graphing (or even when constructing your tables).
2. Avoid the temptation to emphasize your point or position by "adjusting" the vertical axis. This creates a *truncated* graph. The vertical scale is cut off or restricted so that the information becomes distorted. The picture is misleading. This is a practice that the media often use in reporting or sensationalizing stories for the public's (untrained) eye. The axes are exaggerated so that the graph presents dramatic results that really were rather "ho hum." The vertical axis is restricted to a short range, causing overemphasis of the results in either a positive or negative light.

The graph in figure 3.12 reports a "steep decline in SAT values." But look how the vertical scale has been adjusted to begin at 492, distorting the picture. The drop over a three-year period is negligible—from 502 to 496! An initial glance at the graph would cause board of education members to faint—before they could find out the real story in the actual data.

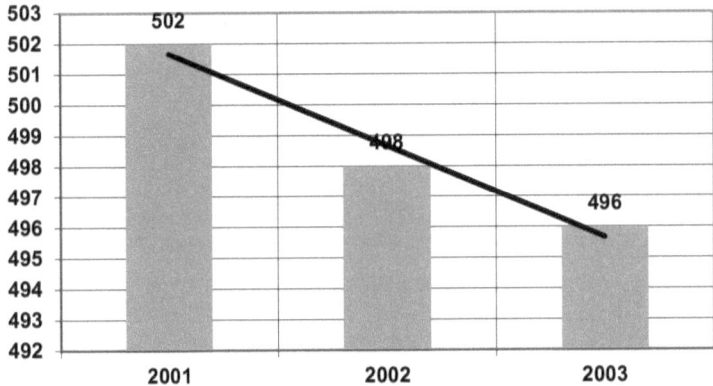

Figure 3.12. "Steep" Decline in SAT Scores over Three Years. *Source: Author developed*

Chapter Summary

Graphs are most beneficial to graduate students because they can provide a summary data sheet when presenting data. However, it is important to keep in mind that a graph is a picture that is helping to tell a story about the data. Those who will be viewing the graph are not as involved in your data and analysis as you are and have other thoughts competing for their attention. Don't waste their time with graphs that are either too simplistic or overly complex. Use graphs judiciously and with deliberation.

CHAPTER FOUR

Means, Medians, and Modes and When to Use Each

The importance of getting to know your data has been discussed. The frequency distributions and the graphing techniques both produce a basic profile of your data set. Taking the time to construct them helps to indicate the characteristics of your data. There are also certain statistics that are generated for the purpose of describing the distributions of your data or the relationships between your variables. They are called *descriptive statistics*. These very useful statistics bring together large amounts of data so they can be presented and comprehended with minimal effort.

Descriptive statistics are widely applied. A good example of real-life applications is the US Census. By using some of the popular descriptive statistics, we get a sense of important characteristics of households in the United States. For example, descriptive statistics that are available in census data may indicate:

- Average household size
- Ethnic, racial, and gender breakdowns
- Employment rates
- Households in poverty
- Characteristics of homeowners and renters
- Per capita income
- Levels of educational attainment

If we had to generate this type of information from looking at raw data, it would be too complex to grasp. Descriptive statistics make it easy to get a sense of what is typical or average.

Measures of *central tendency* represent an important collection of descriptive statistics. These are designed to describe the *central part* of the distribution that you created with your frequency distribution. They tell where most values appear to group, cluster, or fall together—their commonality. In other words, they tell us the average. With one single number you can obtain an accurate picture of your entire distribution. It suggests the profile of a group as a whole and is a concise description. There are three measures of central tendency: the mean, the median, and the mode.

The Mean

The *mean* represents a whole data set with one single number! The mean is the arithmetic average in your distribution of values. To obtain the mean you add up all of the values (Xs) and divide by the total number of values (n) in your distribution. As a rule, your data set should tend to cluster together and not be spread all over. The beauty of the mean is that you utilize each and every value in your data set to calculate it. As a result, it is the most stable measure of central tendency and the one used most often. Since it is an average, you probably have been calculating a mean often in your everyday life. In professional journals, the mean is often noted as M.

Here is a simple example to illustrate the use of the mean. During this past school year, the board of education was contemplating the creation of additional elementary school classroom space. The three neighborhood elementary schools were brimming with children. This was due to recent out-migrations, where families were moving from cities to a more rural location. The board members decided to find out what the average class size was in order to arm themselves with supporting data for overcrowding and ultimately for additional classroom space.

Although class sizes were compiled for all grade levels, the data set for ten third-grade classrooms was reported as follows in table 4.1.

The mean was calculated at 27 students per classroom—larger than what was desirable. Here was the evidence the board of education needed. With just one number representing all 10 classrooms, the board had a solid piece of information.

The mean is a very good measure of central tendency.

Table 4.1. Class Size Data for Third-Grade Classrooms

Third-Grade Classrooms	Class Size
Class 1	15
Class 2	19
Class 3	22
Class 4	29
Class 5	29
Class 6	31
Class 7	31
Class 8	32
Class 9	32
Class 10	33
Mean	27

- It is based on more precise measurement scales such as interval and ratio. Sometimes the ordinal scale is used too. This may occur with rating scales, performance scales, or satisfaction scales where averages are useful. Purists would object to the use of a mean with ordinal data simply because the units of measurement are not exact. However, in many applications, ordinal data is used with the mean because it makes sense. That is the determinant of when to apply the mean to your data—if it is ordinal scaled. If it makes sense in producing good information, by all means use it. (Conversely, no mean can be calculated with nominal scaled variables since the numbers have no meaning.)
- As mentioned before, *all* the values in a data set are used to calculate the mean. This is another advantage.
- Finally, many of the powerful statistical analyses rely on the mean to calculate formulas for statistical significance. The mean has become the queen of central tendency. But this "royal" designation should be avoided if your data set possesses *outliers*.

Outliers

An *outlier* is an extremely high or low value in your distribution. It is *atypical* and does not resemble most of the other numbers in your distribution. It affects the calculation of the mean and makes the mean less representative. While the mean is looking to create a typical value in your data set, the outlier is atypical.

What happens is that outliers cause the mean to shift in the direction of the outlier. If the outlier is a high value, the mean is calculated higher than it should be. If it is a low value, the mean is lower than it should be. Outliers cause your distribution to become skewed. This problem is particularly true if the number of values in your distribution is small.

You can tell if you have outliers in your data set by setting up a frequency distribution and then graphing a frequency polygon. This is another advantage of taking the time to produce frequency distributions and using the graphing techniques. If you have an asymmetrical curve, outliers are hanging around. Some frequency polygons in chapter 3 suffered from the existence of outliers in the data set. The curves in the graphs were irregular as opposed to being balanced in form.

Going back to the example of classroom size, let's alter the data set with three particularly small third-grade classrooms. The data set would look like that in table 4.2.

Table 4.2. Class Size Data for Third-Grade Classrooms with Outliers

Third-Grade Classrooms	Class Size
Class 1	28
Class 2	28
Class 3	29
Class 4	29
Class 5	29
Class 6	31
Class 7	31
Class 8 outlier	9
Class 9 outlier	8
Class 10 outlier	10
Mean	23

Here, the outliers caused the mean to shift down to 23 children per classroom. The presence of the outliers decreased the case for additional classroom space, but it is not a good representation of average class size in your school system. Most class sizes in your data set distribution are around 28 to 31. If you used the mean as the measure of central tendency in this case, you would be presenting an underestimated picture of need.

What should you do? Examine your data through the basic work of developing a frequency distribution, and then use *more than one measure* of central tendency. One of the best, when your data has outliers, is the *median*.

The Median

When there are extreme values or outliers in your distribution, the *median* is the preferred measure of central tendency. The median is the *counting average*. It is simply the midpoint in your distribution of ranked, ordered values. The median can be used with ordinal, interval, and ratio-scaled data. Nominal-scaled data are inappropriate.

To calculate the median, list all of the values in your distribution from the lowest to the highest and then find the *midpoint*—the place where it divides your distribution into equal halves. That is, 50% of all values are above and 50% are below.

The Median: With an Odd Number of Values in Your Distribution

If there is an odd number of values in your distribution, the median is easy to identify. Find the midpoint in the range of high to low values. That midpoint is the median, since half of the values are above it and half are below it. A formula can be used to locate the position in an ordered set of data. It is the

[Median = Number of values plus 1 divided by 2]

If you had 11 values (an odd number), the formula would be (11 + 1) ÷ by 2 = 6. The median would be the sixth value in the set of data where the values are listed in order from lowest to highest.

Here is an example where we have an odd number (11) of values. The midpoint is the sixth value or the exact middle of the distribution. In this distribution, the median is 29, and 29 is an actual value in the data set. There are five values above and below it in table 4.3.

Table 4.3. Median with an Odd Number of Values

Order of values lowest to highest	1st Value	2nd Value	3rd Value	4th Value	5th Value	**6th Value**	7th Value	8th Value	9th Value	10th Value	11th Value
Distribution of 11 values	28	28	29	29	29	**29**	31	31	32	32	33
						Midpoint 50%					

The Median: With an Even Number of Values in Your Distribution

If you have an even number of values, find the two that make the centermost point, and then average them. If you have an even number of values, the median may or may not be an actual value, depending on what the two midpoints are. If the midpoints are identical values, then this is the median. If they need to be averaged, then the median will be an average and not an actual value in your distribution. That is why we say the median is the midpoint, a point not a value.

Here is an example of when this is true. In table 4.2 we had our class size data with the outliers in the group. The outliers shifted our mean down to 23. So, we decide to calculate a median.

The data set consisted of 10 values altogether: an even number of values. We have to find the two midpoints and average them. The 10 values are divided in half—five values on the left and five values on the right. The median is calculated by taking two values at the midpoint or center and calculating a mean. In this case, there is a value of 29 on the left and a value of 31 on the right (see table 4.4).

The formula becomes

[Center point 1 + Center point 2] ÷ 2 = Median

In this example, the application of the formula is [29 + 31] = 60 ÷ 2 = 30 (the Median).

Table 4.4. Median with an Even Number of Values

Order of values lowest to highest	1st Value	2nd Value	3rd Value	4th Value	**5th Value**	**6th Value**	7th Value	8th Value	9th Value	10th Value
Distribution of 10 values	28	28	29	29	**29**	**31**	31	9	8	10

Center points

The median and midpoint of the distribution is 30. However, note that the median is not an actual value in the set of data. As you can see, the median is not affected one bit by the outliers. While the mean was 23, the median of 30 is much more representative of the data set. This is the greatest benefit of using the median. Oddball values in the data set do not affect it. Although the median is not calculated by using all the values in the distribution, as the mean is, the median plays an important role in stating the central tendency of your data set—especially if there are outlier values.

The Mode

The *mode* is an unsophisticated measure of central tendency. It is the most *frequently occurring value* in your distribution. It is a simple but rough statistic to calculate the central tendency of your data. The mode does not need to be calculated. If you look at your frequency distribution, a simple eyeball inspection of your data can tell you which value occurred most often. Look at the tallies or frequencies. It is quick and can be obtained with a glance. We did that in chapter 2 with our first data set of values in table 2.2. We looked at the frequency distribution and could see that the mode was 420 for click rates.

The mode provides little information beyond simply identifying the value in your data set that appears with the greatest frequency. Therefore, it should only be used when you have a large data set of values, and not just a few. A small set of values would not have enough frequency of occurrence to develop a mode. You need many values so that you can be certain which value turned up most often.

When there is one value that occurs with the most frequency in a distribution, we say the distribution is *unimodal* or when graphed it has one hump due to the fact that there is one mode. Many frequency distributions have more than one mode. That is, more than one value turns up at the same high level of frequency. Two modes in a frequency distribution create a *bimodal* frequency distribution. This might occur in a set of data where two groups are very different on the variable measured. If graphed, there would be two humps in the curve or shape. If there are more than two modes, the distribution is called *multimodal* and the graphing shows several humps or curves.

Chapter Summary

Each measure of central tendency has a role to play in descriptive statistics. The mean is the preferred method of calculating the center of your data set. But when outliers emerge, the median is an alternative that is not affected by these unrepresentative values. If you want to get a ballpark feeling for the average, the mode will work with a quick glance at the frequency distribution table. Here is a summary of the three measures and when to use each:

The Mean

- If you want the greatest reliability
- If you will be calculating variability and other statistical computations
- If your distribution has no outliers
- If your data are interval, ratio, or ordinal scaled

The Median

- If your distribution is skewed by outliers
- If your data are interval, ratio, or ordinal scaled

The Mode

- If you need a quick estimate
- If you have interval, ratio, or ordinal scaled data
- If you can eyeball the data from a frequency distribution

CHAPTER FIVE

~

Measuring Variability

An Important Role in Data

So far, a case has been made about the importance of constructing a frequency distribution and plotting the data into a graph for an immediate snapshot of findings. Similarly, the value of the three measures of central tendency was established. They can indicate to us with a single number the general characteristics of our set of data. There is another essential step: measuring the *variability* of data sets. Many times statistics are reported without mention of the variance or spread of values. The media is guilty of this. Doing so can misrepresent data. This is why.

The variance is the manner in which your data are spread in either direction from the center of your distribution. It is important to know whether the values tend to be homogeneous or whether they vary from each other. The measures of variability tell us how representative our mean (M) is. Are the values similar or are they spread out?

For example, look at the glucose levels for patients exposed to prediabetes interventions, either Treatment A or Treatment B, at a hospital. The mean blood sugar level in both cases is 100, so both treatments seem to be equally effective. Closer inspection of the data shows that, while those in Treatment A were very much the same at the end of the treatment, Treatment B had some very high and very low results. For Treatment A, the lowest result was 98 and the highest was 102, not too far apart. For Treatment B, the lowest result was 79 while the highest was 140. The spread or dispersion was great in Treatment B, where there was high variability. Conversely, the low variability in Treatment A was evident from the similar values. There are practical implications for Treatment B patients that would be overlooked if just the mean was used to profile outcome data. Please see table 5.1.

Table 5.1. Two Treatments with Similar Means

Patients in Treatment A	Patients in Treatment B
98	140
102	80
99	79
100	100
99	100
100	79
102	80
98	140
Mean = 100	Mean = 100

There are several descriptive statistics that measure variability: the range, the variance, and the standard deviation.

The Range

The *range* is a very simple statistic and the most unsophisticated measure of variability. In this regard, it possesses characteristics analogous to the *mode* in central tendency. It is a rough estimate, quickly computed, but not tremendously stable. This is because it is computed with only two values: the highest value and the lowest value in your distribution of values. You subtract one from the other. The range for Treatment A would be 4 (102 – 98) while the range for Treatment B would be 61 (140 – 79). Even this crude measure of variability is very helpful in providing us with information that the mean value for Treatment B is not stable.

The range is influenced by the size of your data set. The larger the data set, the greater the likelihood of extreme values because you have more potential for outliers. This is a limitation of the range; outliers affect it. Since you are using only two values in your data set to calculate the range, if there is an outlier at either end, it will influence the calculation.

Variability and Graphs

Graphs, discussed in chapter 3, are quite useful in initially determining the variability in your distribution. The *shape* of the frequency polygons and histograms that are constructed from the frequency distribution can tell us the story about the spread of values at a glance. This is another asset of the frequency distribution (and their respective graphs), and a further reason to use them in getting to know your data set.

If the hump or curve in your graph is markedly flat, the values are spread out; there is a great deal of variability. Subjects are not alike. This type of curve, called *platykurtic*, means that your values are spread out around the mean value of the distribution. On the other hand, if the hump or curve in your graph is peaked and tight, there is little spread in values; the variability is low. Subjects are alike. This type of curve, called *leptokurtic*, means that your values are very close to the mean value of the distribution. (Please refer to the corresponding figures in chapter 3.)

Another example is illustrated in two graphs that display the number of pounds that bank employees lost during a Get Healthy Competition. The intervention group participated in a special exercise and nutrition program and the comparison group did not.

For both groups the mean number of pounds lost was 6 pounds. As you can see, employees in the intervention group performed similarly. The members lost between 4.5 and 8.5 pounds each. On the other hand, the comparison group lost between 1 pound and 11 pounds. In fact, the range was 10 (11 – 1) for the comparison group and only 4 (8 – 4) for the intervention group! This difference in spread of pounds lost is different between the two groups. But the mean is 6 pounds for each group. Please refer to figures 5.1 and 5.2, which present visuals that indicate the variability or spread of values.

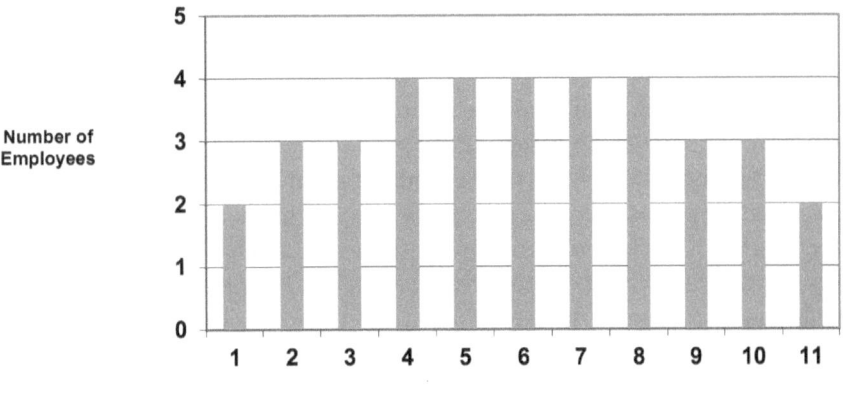

Figure 5.1. Comparison Group. *Source: Author developed*

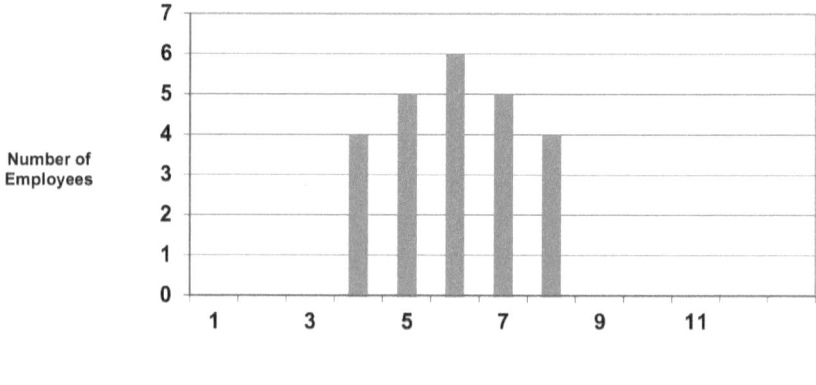

Figure 5.2. Intervention Group. *Source: Author developed*

The shapes of the curves immediately indicate the dispersion or spread of values. For the comparison group the shape of the curve is flat (*platykurtic*). The message from the graph is that values are spread out around the mean. To claim that most bank employees were performing as well without the special program is false. For the intervention group the shape of the curve is peaked (*leptokurtic*). The mean is an excellent measure of central tendency because there is little spread. It would be safe to conclude that most intervention group employees were more successful than the comparison group even though mean values are the same. If a statistical procedure were applied to these data, there likely would be a significant difference between the intervention and comparison groups.

Variance and Standard Deviation

There are two additional measures of variability: the *variance* and the *standard deviation*. Both are much better indicators of dispersion in your data set than the range. The reason is that they use all of the values in the data set in their calculation (just as the mean does). While the mode and the range have similar traits (quick, unsophisticated), the mean and the variance/standard deviation are very much alike (precise, reliable). They are the kings of variability as the mean is the queen of central tendency. In addition, each of these statistics relies on more precise measurement scales such as interval and ratio. (Some use the ordinal scale but there is a trade-off in precision.)

The formulas for calculating both the variance and the standard deviation can be found in any math or statistics book. However, if you are using a statistical software package like SPSS, these will be calculated for you.

Conceptually, each of these statistics is based upon how much each value in your data set deviates from the mean, and then putting the deviation values into a formula for computation. The variance is the standard deviation squared, and the standard deviation is the square root of the variance. They are more or less "siblings" in the realm of variance. The symbol for reporting the variance is "sigma squared" (σ^2). The symbol for standard deviation is SD or sigma (σ). These are what you might see in professional journals.

Because both the variance and standard deviation are calculated by deviations from the mean in your data set, their value is tremendous. With one single number, you can tell whether most of the values in your data set cluster closely around the mean or are spread out. The larger the standard deviation, the more spread out are your values in your data set.

For example, let's consider customer satisfaction scores over a two-year period for a restaurant chain where 900 was the highest possible score. Last year they had a mean of 600 and a SD of 50. This year they had a mean of 610 and SD of 100. Our mean (M) customer satisfaction scores rose from 600 to 610. What appears to be good news for our restaurant chain is in fact a hidden problem. The standard deviation of 100 shows outlier values have shifted the mean upward and artificially created the image that all of our values were rising. While we can celebrate the seemingly good news this year, it puts a strain on next year when we have to explain to the CEO why the values are back down to (or below) 600. If the standard deviation were calculated in addition to the mean, there would be a more accurate presentation of our restaurant's performance.

Here is sound advice: *Whenever you report the mean, you should report the standard deviation.* They are the statistical couple. The standard deviation tells you a great deal: how representative your mean is as a measure of central tendency for your data set.

Look at the data for the *number of motor vehicle accidents* occurring in three towns of about the same size and demographic profiles over a five-year period (see table 5.2):

Table 5.2. Motor Vehicle Accidents by Town

Town	Mean Per Year	Standard Deviation
Litchfield	60	2
Torrington	60	1
Winsted	60	15

At face value three towns have the exact same number of accidents among residents: 60. So, you assume that this is typical or average. However, the standard deviations tell a very different story. For Torrington and Litchfield, the means are very representative of the average. The *SD* is small for both. If you actually drew a frequency polygon from the frequency distribution data per month, these two towns would have leptokurtic curves. The values would be close to the mean.

But this is not true for Winsted. This town has a greater spread of values around its mean of 60, as signified by the standard deviation of 15. The frequency polygon for Winsted data would be flat, not peaked. And actually, the median might be the better measure of central tendency in this case.

Normal Curves or Normal Distributions

The standard deviation is one of the most valuable tools that graduate students have at their disposal. One of its primary uses is in helping to interpret data. To fully understand its value, a discussion of *the normal curve* is necessary.

Most of the data that we use is thought to be *normally distributed*. This means that if we constructed a frequency distribution and then graphed a frequency polygon, the hump or curve would be symmetrical. When graphed, the frequency distribution resembles a bell, which means that there are a few values on either end of the hump or curve; most values are in the middle.

Area under the Normal Curve

A normal distribution creates a *bell-shaped* curve or frequency polygon. These are some characteristics of the normal curve:

1. It has one mode (unimodal)
2. The mean, median, and mode are exactly the same number
3. It is symmetrical and bell-shaped

When you draw a normal curve, you observe these characteristics. The normal curve, when drawn in most statistics books, has ordinates or vertical lines from the top of the curve to the baseline. When you look at the picture of a normal curve, visualize thousands of people standing under the curve; imagine faces looking at you. This is what the normal curve is representing—data of individuals on whatever variables you are examining.

In the normal curve, the vertical lines are drawn from the top of the curve to the baseline at 0 and at numbers 1, 2, and 3 *to the left and to the right of 0*. Zero (0) represents the mean value or dead center. These vertical lines mark off areas under the curve and represent standard deviation units (1, 2, and 3) or distance from the mean. The standard deviation (SD) units act like a ruler and divide up the area under the normal curve as illustrated in figure 5.3.

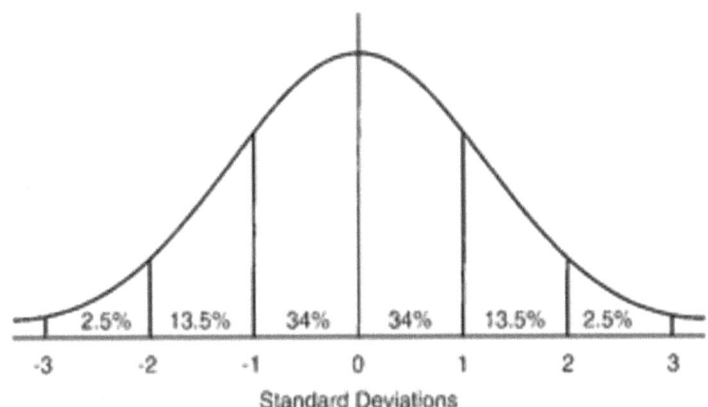

Figure 5.3. Normal Curve, Standard Deviations, and Areas Under the Curve. *Source: Author developed*

The base of the normal curve is divided into six units with three SD above and three SD below the mean. Entries within the graph indicate the proportion of the total area (or number of values) that falls into each of the six segments or demarcations. These are the proportions of area under the SD cutoffs:

- between the mean (0) and +1 SD units are 34.1% of all values
- between the mean (0) and −1 SD units are 34.1% of all values
- between ±1 SD are 68% of all values

- between +1 SD and +2 SD units are 13.5% of all values
- between −1 SD and −2 SD units are 13.5% of all values
- between ±2 SD are 95% of all values

- between +2 SD and +3 SD units are 2.5% of all values
- between −2 SD and −3 SD units are 2.5% of all values
- between ±3 SD are 99% of all values

Since we know that the mean is dead center, it is at the 50th percentile mark. The next bit of information is important in interpreting values:

- *One standard deviation above the mean* is an area of 34%. This indicates that if your value is 1 SD above the mean, you are higher than 84% of all other values in the distribution (50% plus 34%).
- *One standard deviation below the mean* is an area of 34%. This indicates that if your value is 1 SD below the mean, you are higher than only 16% (50% – 34%).
- *One standard deviation above and below the mean* is an area of 68%. Over two-thirds are within one standard deviation of the mean (±1 #SD). If you look at the normal curve and pretend again that people are standing underneath it, then this is very logical. It is where *most values fall*, creating the large hump.
- *Two standard deviations above the mean* cover an area of 48%. Between the center (0) and +1 SD there is 34% of the area under the curve. Between +1 SD and +2 SD there is 14% of the area under the curve. As you can see, the further you get from the center, the less area there is under the curve. This is because most values are in the center where the hump is. Again, think of people standing underneath the curve. If you obtain a value that is two standard deviations above the mean, that is a select few. This value is better than 98% of all others (50% + 48%).
- *Two standard deviations below the mean* cover an area of 48%. Between the center and –1 SD there is 34% of the area under the curve. Between –1 SD and –2 SD there is 14% of the area under the curve. If you get a value that is two standard deviations below the mean, this is in the minority. The value is better than only 2% of all others (50% – 48%).
- *Two standard deviations above and below the mean* is an area of 95%. If you look at the normal curve and pretend again that people are standing underneath it to create the hump in it, then the percentage of 95% is very logical. Almost all people perform within two standard deviation units of the mean (±2 SD).

The standard deviation units, together with the percentage of area under the normal curve, can be used to determine the relative position of values above and below the mean. The information is defined as the "distance from the mean." Extremely useful, this is why.

All standardized measurement tools have means and standard deviations reported. You can compare your data to the national norms. The normal curve gives you the ability to make a call on where your sample of subjects stands in relation to all others. This is because the percentiles under the normal curve indicate the relative position of those falling above and below a certain designation.

Standard or Z Scores

A *standard* or *z score* is another useful tool. Its symbol is lowercase z. It tells you how many standard deviations a raw score is from the mean. You calculate a z score by taking a subject's raw score (X) minus the mean (M) and then dividing it by the standard deviation (SD) of your data. This is your z score. If the z value is negative, then your z score is below the mean. If it is positive, it is above the mean. If it is zero, it is the mean.

For example, the IQ test has a mean of 100 and a standard deviation of 15. Your IQ was 130. If you apply the formula, your standard score would be +2.00 or two standard deviations above the mean. Referring back to area under the normal curve, your score would be higher than 98% of those who took the IQ test.

Most statistics books have a table that helps you convert your raw data to z values, and some statistical programs will even do the conversion for you.

Skewed Distributions

Before closing this chapter, we need to address the fact that often our distributions or data sets are not normally distributed. Don't panic. This is the case more often than not with thesis or dissertation data. Just as a review, *normal distribution curves* have the following characteristics:

- They are unimodal—having one mode only.
- The maximum height is at the mean where the zero (0) or vertical axis touches the top of the curve.
- The mean, median, and mode are equal.
- They are symmetrical and bell-shaped. One half approximates the other half, a mirror image.
- There are one-half of the values on one side and one-half on the opposite side of the mean.
- There are three standard deviations above and below the mean.
- They assume an infinite number of values underneath the curve, so the two tails at either end do not touch the abscissa.
- They can be either platykurtic (flat) or leptokurtic (peaked), as well as in between.

On the other hand, we could have *positively or negatively skewed distributions*. How do we know? If values are clustered near the middle in a frequency distribution with a few values at the high and low ends, then it is pretty much a normal distribution. If there are concentrations of values on either the high or low ends, then the distribution is skewed. Here are the hints.

- Our frequency distributions will confirm this because they will have outliers in them.
- The mean, median, and mode will not be equal.
- The frequency polygon will extend outward either left of right. This extension is called a *tail*.

(Please refer to the figures in chapter 3.)

Positively Skewed Distributions
The *tail* of the curve tells you what kind of skew you have. If the tail is to the right, you have a *positively skewed curve*. With a positively skewed curve, the hump of the curve is toward the left. Remember when graphing frequency polygons, the left side of the horizontal axis begins with the lowest values. Because the hump is in this vicinity, your distribution has many low values. The few high values, represented in the tail area, skew it. These "outlier" high values pull the mean upward; the average is overrepresented. The mean *shifts* toward the outlier. In a positively skewed distribution, the mode is at the peak of the distribution. The mean is off to the right and the median in between.

An example of a positively skewed distribution would be results of testing intended to tap an elite few. The test would be extremely difficult, yielding very few high values. Testing to become a Navy Seal or a Rhodes Scholar might be examples of such tests. The few that did well would be the values on the tail and those who did not do well would be the large hump. Those in the tail of the curve would qualify or be selected because the program targets those with extremely high results.

Negatively Skewed Distributions
If the tail is to the left, you have a *negatively skewed curve*. With a negatively skewed curve, the hump or curve shows where most values are falling. In this case they are at the higher end of the horizontal axis: the hump or curve is on the right side of the frequency polygon. The few low values, represented in the tail area, skew it. These "outlier" low values pull the mean downward; the average is underrepresented. The mean *shifts* toward the outlier. In a negatively skewed distribution, the mode remains at the peak, the mean is off to the left and the median is in between.

An example of a negatively skewed distribution would be values on an easy test where most did well. A driver's education exam should have a negatively skewed distribution. Most people pass it. Negatively skewed distributions may be used to identify areas of need: academic, physical, psychological, nutritional. You would be looking at those values in the tail to identify those with high levels of need. This is not the majority; it is the minority who have some kind of need that you want to identify from those who do not have that need.

Chapter Summary

Reporting only part of the story about your data set occurs when measures for variance are missing. You are looking at part of the information puzzle but leaving off an important dimension. If your thesis or dissertation research hinges on descriptive statistics, then using both central tendency measures and measures of variation will be considered vital.

CHAPTER SIX

Random Sampling and Other Useful Sampling Strategies

Time is at a premium for graduate students. Although it probably was never conceived in this fashion, statistics is a tool that saves time. It allows you to conduct your research without spending many extra hours. Why is this so? Statistics are based on samples. We have often heard the term *random sample* or *scientific sample*. Yet few of us really know what this designation means or understand how valuable it is.

Populations and Samples

The term *population* makes us think of all of the people in our town, region, state, or country, and their respective characteristics such as gender, age, marital status, ethnicity, race, religion, and so forth. In statistics, the term *population* takes on a slightly different meaning.

The *population* in statistics includes all members of a defined group on which we are collecting information. The operative descriptor is "all": all children under the age of five, senior executives, first offenders, hospital patients, or the entire community of households in whatever geographic circle we are focused. The population in our statistical study is defined by the who (target group) and the where (the geographic boundary in which this group exists).

A part of the population is called a *sample*. Samples are studied to obtain valuable information about the larger group called the population. Once we define our population, we can take a sample of the population to conduct our statistics. A sample is a subset or subgroup of our population. It is a proportion of the population, a slice of it and all its characteristics. A sample is a group that actually *possesses the same characteristics* as the population—if it is drawn randomly. This may be hard for you to believe, but it is true.

Randomly drawn samples must have two characteristics:

1. Every person has an equal chance to be selected for the sample.
2. Selection of one person is independent of the selection of another person.

We use samples all the time to represent the whole. We take a sample of exotic food, maybe a bite or two to see if it pleases our palette. We use a sample of new software that comes in the mail to see if it really works as well as the manufacturer purports it does. We take a sample of client references to see if the consultant is as good as the proposal suggests. We visit a sample of classrooms to determine if behavioral issues are increasing. We sample some of the households in our community to see what languages are spoken at home.

Why not use the entire population to draw our conclusions? The short answer is it is a waste of time. For most purposes we can obtain suitable accuracy, quickly and inexpensively, from a sample. Assessing all individuals may be impossible, impractical, expensive, or even inaccurate. It is usually not feasible to include an *entire* population in a study except if the number of those in our population is small and manageable. Furthermore, statistics make it unnecessary. A sign of ineptitude in data management is using an entire population when a sample will provide the same results. You save money, time, make fewer mistakes, and achieve the same end.

What is great about random samples is that you can generalize to the population that you are interested in. If you randomly sample 300 households in your community, you can generalize to the 50,000 households that live there. If you match some of the demographic characteristics of the 300 with the 50,000, you will see that they are surprisingly similar. Technically speaking, if you calculated a mean for these 300 randomly selected households and then drew another sample of 300 different households from the same population as the first, your mean values (M) would be the same. This is the beauty of random samples. If drawn scientifically, they represent the entire population in which you are interested.

Many a doubting Thomas will still be skeptical about whether a sample can truly represent the population. This is understandable. Yet if properly conducted, sampling does work. Think about all the polls reported in the media. They do not survey all of the nation's households. Instead, a random sample is drawn and surveyed. The results are pretty accurate. If you would like to get a feeling for the size of samples that represent entire populations, please refer to Krejcie and Morgan (1970; see source for Table 6.1). Table 6.1 suggests the great benefit that randomly selected samples afford. The larger the population size, the smaller the sample. However, for smaller samples, you must use almost the entire population. (Population size is noted by uppercase "N" and sample size by lower case "n.")

Table 6.1. Random Sample Sizes (*n*) Required for Population (*N*) Representation

Population Size (N)	Sample Size (n)
50	44
100	80
500	217
1,000	278
1,500	306
3,000	341
5,000	357
10,000	375
50,000	381
100,000	384

Source: R. V. Krejcie and D. W. Morgan 1970. "Determining Sample Size for Research Activities." *Educational and Psychological Measurements*, 30, 607–10.

Samples must be drawn according to scientific principles—with precision and accuracy. There is a price to having a *truly representative* sample. But the process is quite simple and methodological. If you follow the steps, you will find that the characteristics of your population are the same as those of your sample. This is a good check on the validity of your sample. If the percentages on some of the demographics are known about your population, then the same demographics will appear in the sample. This is a good test and a very convincing piece of information for those skeptics.

Steps for Drawing Simple Random Samples

Here are the steps for drawing a random sample, if you choose to use a random sample in your graduate research. It may not be feasible to do this, but it is important to know the steps in the process if you opt for this sampling procedure.

1. The first step in drawing a random sample is to identify all the members in your population. You must be able to list them in what is called a *sampling frame*. The frame should have the names without order to them and be nonoverlapping (no duplicates). Alphabetizing the list by surname is a way to ensure a random order in the sampling frame. Your computer can sort alphabetically based on the last name, if surname is entered into a database as a separate field. One reason that you need to ensure random order of names is that some lists cluster them by neighborhood location, housing type, income, or some other grouping. This precludes their "equal chance" of being selected.
2. Give each name an identification number. Start with "1" and continue.
3. Decide the size for your sample. You can use the table (see table 6.1), or whatever you believe is right, in order to believe in the results you obtain. As a rule of thumb, use as large a sample as possible. Whenever you are calculating means, percentages, or other statistics, the population is being estimated. Statistics calculated from large samples are more accurate than those from small samples. Large samples give the principle of randomness a chance to work.
4. Get a *Table of Random Numbers* (table 6.3 displays a partial one). Many are located at the end of statistical or mathematical textbooks. The Table of Random Numbers contains numbers generated mechanically so that there is no discernable order or system to them. Each digit gets an equal representation. The Table of Random Numbers consists of rows and columns of numbers arranged at random so that they can be used at any point by reading in any direction left or right, up or down.

We are now ready to draw our random sample. Here is our sampling frame of 20 members of our population who are behavioral health counselors. The director of the behavioral health clinic wants to select five counselors for an overnight stay in the clinic with teens who are inpatients. In order to be fair in the selection process, the director uses random sampling and lists the 20 counselors' names in alphabetical order and assigns an ID number to each from 1 through 20. Table 6.2 has the sampling frame.

The director knows that the largest ID number has two digits (20). So, they are going to need a two-digit column in the Table of Random Numbers. They put their finger down at any place in the Table of Random numbers. This is their starting point. They have to decide in advance whether they would use two digits going up, down, left, or right.

Table 6.2. Sampling Frame

ID	Name
1	Annie
2	Ellen
3	Emily
4	Estelle
5	James
6	Jessica
7	Jose
8	Juan
9	Kaleen
10	Lia
11	Loren
12	Maria
13	Mary
14	McKenzie
15	Michelle
16	Miguel
17	Olivia
18	Raphaelle
19	Rebecca
20	Tanya

Table 6.3 is a Table of Random Numbers—just for the point of illustration. In boldface is the director's starting point of 37. They do not have an ID number that is 37 and so they proceed down: 37, 81, 89, and come to 06. ID #6 is the first ID number that is within the band of between 1 and 20. This is the first member of the random sample, and it is *Jessica*. They continue 82, 56, 96, 66, 46 until they come up with the next ID #13, *Mary*. Their three last members of the sample are ID #8 (*Juan*), ID #5 (*James*), and ID #4 (*Estelle*). They now have five randomly selected members: Jessica, Mary, Juan, James, and Estelle who will be staying overnight with the teens.

The Old Way Works Too
For such a small sampling frame, we could have done it the old way by drawing five names out of a bowl that had all 20 names in it. And you can draw a random sample that way instead of using the Table of Random Numbers. You simply put all names in a container and thoroughly mix them up. If you have 1,000 names in the bowl and want a sample of 100, draw the first name out. That is the first person in the sample. Mix up the names. If you don't do this, then the name at the bottom will have less of a chance of being selected. After mixing, draw the next name and continue until you get 100.

Table 6.3. Table of Random Numbers (Partial)

53	74	23	99	67	61	32	28	69	84	94	62	67	86	24
63	38	06	86	54	99	00	65	26	94	02	82	90	23	07
35	30	58	21	46	06	72	17	**10**	94	25	21	31	75	96
63	43	36	82	69	65	51	18	**37**	88	61	38	44	12	45
98	25	37	55	26	01	91	82	**81**	46	74	71	12	94	97
02	63	21	17	69	71	50	80	**89**	56	38	15	70	11	48
64	55	22	21	82	48	22	28	**06**	00	61	54	13	43	91
85	07	26	13	89	01	10	07	82	**04**	59	63	69	36	03
58	54	16	24	15	51	54	44	82	00	62	61	65	04	69
34	85	27	84	87	61	48	64	56	26	90	18	48	13	26
03	92	18	27	46	57	99	16	96	56	30	33	72	85	22
62	95	30	27	59	37	75	41	66	48	86	97	80	61	45
08	45	93	15	22	60	21	75	46	91	98	77	27	85	42
07	08	55	18	40	45	44	75	**13**	90	24	94	96	61	02
01	85	89	95	66	51	10	19	34	88	15	84	97	19	75
72	84	71	14	35	19	11	58	49	26	50	11	17	17	76
88	78	28	16	84	13	52	53	94	53	75	45	69	30	96
45	17	75	65	57	28	40	19	72	12	25	12	74	75	67
96	76	28	12	54	22	01	11	94	25	71	96	16	16	88
43	31	67	72	30	24	02	94	**08**	63	38	32	36	66	02
50	44	66	44	21	66	06	58	**05**	62	68	15	54	35	02
22	66	22	15	86	26	63	75	41	99	58	42	36	72	24
96	24	40	14	51	23	22	30	88	57	95	67	47	29	83
31	73	91	61	19	60	20	72	93	48	98	57	07	23	69
78	60	73	99	84	43	89	94	36	45	56	69	47	07	41

This works the exact same way as using the Table of Random Numbers and is useful if your sample is small in size.

There are also free random number generators on the internet that you can use: two are www.random.org and www.randomizer.org.

Other Useful Sampling Strategies

Simple random sampling is the premier way to draw your sample. There are other sampling strategies that are very useful as well. Many books on sampling provide more in-depth information about the processes and the benefits. Here is a summary of a few procedures that you can consider.

Systematic sampling is a cost-effective and often-used sampling strategy. Again, you must have a population sampling frame listing names in random order that is nonoverlapping. Determine both the size of the population and the size of the sample you want to work with. Then, divide the sample size (n) into the population (N) size to get your *key number*, symbolized as "k."

- For example, if you had a population of 1,500 (N) and needed to have a sample of 306 (n), *the key number* (k) would be 5.
- Then, you would randomly pick any number between 1 and 5. Let's say you picked "4." That is your first ID number. ID #4 is the first member of your sample from the list of 1,500.
- Then, systematically add 5 (your key number) to the first ID number of 4 and you get #9. ID #9 is the second member of your sample. Continue adding your key number.
- The next ID number is ID #14, then ID #19, ID #24, ID #29 until you get your sample size up to the 306 you intended.

You might use systematic sampling to select a sample of households in your community for a housing survey. Town government might have the listing already available, in random order and with ID numbers in sequence. This saves you time and labor. If the town will give you a set of mailing labels or email addresses, then it will be all the better.

Cluster sampling is exactly what its title implies. You randomly select clusters, or groups, in a population instead of individuals. This would work if a state wanted to sample all third graders on their writing skills. They would randomly select third grade classrooms from all third-grade classrooms in the state. Each of those classrooms selected would have 100% of the students in that classroom in the sample. The sampling unit or cluster is the third-grade classroom not the individual student. Sometimes, this is a more practical effort than selecting individuals. Each member of the cluster has an equal chance of being selected. The random selection of the clusters provides estimates of the population. This is a good cost reduction technique.

Stratified sampling is used when the population is heterogeneous, and it is important to represent the different strata or subpopulations. There is a proportional representation of strata in the sample—proportional to the population strata. We divide the entire population into strata (groups) to obtain groups of people that are more or less equal in some respect. Then, select a random sample from each stratum. This ensures that no group is missed and improves the precision of our estimates. This might be used with different racial/ethnic groups if we wanted to ensure that our sample included a proportional representation of African Americans, Asians, and Latinos in addition to the Caucasians that might predominate our demographic pool.

There are three *nonrandom sampling strategies* that graduate students should consider using, especially if you have descriptive or nonexperimental designs. These sampling strategies are convenience, purposive, and snowball sampling. Many times, random sampling strategies are impossible to undertake at the graduate level. These three strategies are options to consider.

Convenience samples, exactly what the name suggests, are often what we have to use because of reality. It is a nonrandom sampling technique. This is a useful sampling strategy because you cannot draw a sample, yet you have a group that is accessible, is representative of the target population of interest, and available. Use what you have with the honest acknowledgment that there are limitations. If you proceed to collect data with respect to some systematic, thoughtful process, it is better than predicting with some impractical power analysis what your sample size will be—and then failing to achieve it.

Purposive sampling, another nonrandom sampling technique, is used when the researcher seeks out subjects with specific characteristics to participate in the research study. This might be done if your study involved parents of daycare children. You might seek permission from daycare centers to ask their parents to participate in the research.

Snowball sampling, another nonrandom sampling technique, asks each research participant who volunteers for your study to identify one or more others who might be willing to participate. This might be used if you were studying African American female executives. The sample's network might produce more volunteers to add to your sample. There might be just a few whom you identify initially but over the course of the research, those few might help to identify like members of hard-to-find populations.

Chapter Summary

Except when the population of interest is small, it is imprudent to survey an entire population. Sampling strategies are available for your use. By using simple random, systematic, cluster, stratified, convenience, purposive or snowball sampling procedures we can get a handle on what we need to know, save time, and get the thesis or dissertation completed expeditiously. One of the most important uses of samples is that they afford us the opportunity to make inferences without spending a fortune in time and money to do so.

CHAPTER SEVEN

Stating Hypotheses and Hypothesis Testing

Descriptive statistics, which describe our data, are very useful. Other statistics are also very useful but take a little more comprehension in implementation. They are called *inferential statistics*. This is because we can draw conclusions or inferences from them.

In the course of your graduate school research, you pose guesses or hunches that you believe to be true. In order to tell whether these hypotheses are true or false, you have to subject them to a test. You may draw a randomly selected sample from the population of interest, compute statistics on the sample, and test whether the hunch is true or false. Central to the discussion of inferential statistics is the concept of *probability*. When your statistical analysis reveals that the probability is rare that your statistical result is due to chance alone, we call this a *statistically significant* result. It means that our observed outcome is so unique that it is unlikely to have occurred by luck.

The role of the sample, discussed in the previous chapter, is essential to the process and makes the task of inferring a possibility. The inferential statistics most commonly used by graduate students to draw these conclusions include t-test, one-way analysis of variance, chi-square analysis, and correlational techniques including regression, among many others. These will be discussed in this book since they are considered to be user-friendly, pragmatic, and applicable in research conducted by most graduate students.

Hypothesis Testing

Hypotheses are *suppositions presumed to be true*. Because of the importance of posing these hypotheses, it is crucial to accept those that are true, and reject those that are false. But how do we do this?

All research, whether it is in the graduate program or in the laboratory, begins with the research question or hypothesis. It is always stated in the null (negative) and is called the *null hypothesis*. This is because it is incumbent on you, the researcher, to prove something is indeed true. It is similar to the philosophy in the courtroom: innocent until proven guilty. The onus of proof is on you to prove that the null is false. Technically speaking, the word *hypothesis* is derived from a Greek word that means "an assumption subject to verification." The symbol for the null hypothesis is H_0. Basically, there are two types of null hypotheses: one that tests for differences and one that tests for *relationships* between or among variables.

Null Hypotheses That Test for Differences

The first type tests for *differences*. Two null hypotheses that test for differences are presented below as an illustration of how to state them correctly. Corresponding examples follow each.

- There is *no difference* between two groups on some variable, as represented by their mean scores. Example: there is no difference between newly hired and long-term employees with respect to their levels of job satisfaction.
- There is *no difference* among three or more groups on some variable, as represented by their mean scores. Example: there is no difference among Asian, African American, Latino, and Caucasian lawyers with respect to their annual salaries.

Directional Null Hypotheses
Sometimes a null hypothesis that tests for differences takes a courageous step and predicts the *direction* of the difference. This is called a *directional null hypothesis*. Instead of stating a nondirectional null like this, "There is no difference between newly hired and long-term employees with respect to their level of job satisfaction," you would state a directional null like this, "Newly hired employees do not have higher levels of job satisfaction than long-term employees do." The basis for this *directional* guess should be your knowledge base, evidence in the professional literature or your own experience, and not

be a superficial guess. You are actually stating which mean will be greater when you calculate your statistics.

In this case, you really believe that newly hired employees have higher levels of job satisfaction than long-term employees do. Remember that the hypothesis must still be stated in the opposite of what you think is true. It has to be stated in the null (which you really think is false). Then you have to prove it to be false. When we accept the null (or fail to reject the null), we are saying that our results are not statistically significant. When we reject the null (or the null is false) we are saying that our results are statistically significant and likely due to factors or conditions other than chance.

Null Hypotheses That Test for Relationships
The second type of null hypothesis tests for *relationships* between or among variables.

- There is *no relationship* between one variable and another variable. Example: there is no relationship between hours of sleep and work productivity.
- There is *no relationship* between one variable and several other variables. Example: there is no relationship between work productivity and hours of sleep, age and coffee consumption.

For practical utility this book will focus on these two types of null hypotheses: those that test for differences and those that test for relationships.

Alternative Hypotheses
If hypothesis testing shows that the null hypothesis is false, and is rejected, the *alternative* hypothesis is stated. The symbol for the alternative hypothesis is H_a. It asserts that the opposite of what the null hypothesis stated is true. Almost always, graduate students believe that the alternative hypothesis is true and that the null is false. But statistics are used to prove it. For the previous null hypotheses, these are the corresponding alternative hypotheses:

- There is a difference between newly hired and long-term employees with respect to their levels of job satisfaction.
- There is a difference among Asian, African American, Latino, and Caucasian lawyers with respect to their annual salaries.
- There is a relationship between hours of sleep and work productivity.
- There is a relationship between work productivity and hours of sleep, age, and coffee consumption.

Probability Levels

How do graduate students determine whether a null hypothesis should be accepted or rejected? Data are collected and statistics are executed. But the key is the *probability value* associated with the statistical procedure that allows the decision to be made. The probability value is also called the *p* value. It is obtained once you execute your statistical analysis. You compare the significance level you chose with the *p* value you obtained to determine whether there are statistically significant results.

Probability applies exclusively to the likely occurrence of a future event. In statistics, probability provides a quantitative measurement of the likelihood that event will occur. In other words, probability is used to measure the certainty or uncertainty of the outcome of an event. If it is sure to occur, the probability is 100%. If it will never occur, the probability is 0%. A probability of .50 means the event should occur 50% of the time. Any event that may or may not occur has a probability of between 0 and 1.00.

Professional journals often state with the results from a statistical procedure that "the probability level is less than .05" ($p < .05$). This means that observed difference is likely to be real rather than having occurred by chance. Or the statistical results may have occurred by chance only five out of 100 times. Although somewhat arbitrary, the probability level is the magnitude of error that one is willing to accept in making the decision to reject the null hypothesis.

The conventional levels for rejecting the null hypothesis are either .05 or .01. One (.01) is more conservative than the other (.05) because with .01 there is less willingness to have results due to chance alone; only one time in 100 will results be due to chance. A .05 significance level is more generous in accepting a statement as true. A very conservative significance level is .001 or one time in 1,000. This may be used in scientific studies such as drug efficacy. For graduate students, the commonly accepted significance levels for rejecting the null hypothesis are .05 and .01.

As a note, the significance levels must be chosen a priori. This is a Latin term meaning "in advance." Decide the significance level early on, before collecting data, and accept it when the statistical testing is completed. It is unethical to choose the conservative .01 significance level and then find out that statistical significance would have occurred if the more liberal choice of .05 was made.

Type I and Type II Errors
It is true that the selection of significance levels (.05, .01) comes with the chance of making errors. These are called Type I and Type II errors.

Type I Errors

A Type I error is when the null is rejected when it was actually true, concluding falsely that there were differences or relationships when there were none. This can be problematic when someone else replicates the study and the results do not hold up.

Making a Type I error is based on the level of statistical significance. If a .05 significance level was selected, then five times out of 100 the results will be due to chance. Unfortunately, one of the five times occurred. A more conservative significance level is .01 where only one time out of 100 the results will be due to chance alone. A liberal significance level is .10 where 10 times out of 100 chance results are OK. This level is not practiced in most graduate student research and can largely contribute to Type I errors.

The Bonferroni Technique

When performing multiple significance tests in graduate research studies, there is the risk of making a Type I error. A way to reduce this risk is by using the Bonferroni correction to adjust the probability level. To do this, simply divide the significance level by the number of significance tests you are performing. If using a significance level of $p \leq .05$ and there are two significance tests in the study, the significance level becomes .025 (.05 ÷ 2 = .025) needed to reject the null hypotheses. It is more conservative, but it will reduce the likelihood of making a Type 1 error. Your calculated p value must be less than .025 to reject the null.

For example, if you measured the levels of stress (pre- and post-) and anxiety (pre- and post-) for college freshmen, you would have two hypotheses with two corresponding significance tests. The probability level would be adjusted by the Bonferroni technique from .05 to .025. This would make it harder both to reject the null, and concurrently avoid a Type I error.

Type II Errors

A Type II error occurs when accepting the null when it was in fact false, concluding that there were no differences or relationships when in fact there were. If the null should have been rejected, but it was not, the maintenance of the status quo may be a mistake. For example, you use conservative significance level such as .01 to determine if a pre-K program attendance had an effect on academic performance for first graders. The statistical result suggests no impact when in fact there was one. Not rejecting the null (accepting the status quo) might limit funding for a program with important benefits because of the choice of a conservative significance level.

Power to Reject the Null Hypothesis

One-Tailed and Two-Tailed Tests of Statistical Significance

With nondirectional null hypotheses, a graduate student is only suggesting that there will be a difference in mean score results. Which mean (M) will be higher is not speculated. In the case of a nondirectional null hypothesis, a two-tailed test of significance is used. If there is a prediction of which mean will be higher and which will be lower, then a one-tailed test of significance is used. This might be the case if you are predicting that managers who have an MBA will have higher employee retention than managers who do not have an MBA. When stating a directional hypothesis, a one-tailed test of significance is used.

This may seem like a lot of mumbo jumbo, but all it means is simply this: a directional hypothesis is a serious commitment for someone to make; they are predicting which mean score (M) of the groups they are comparing will be higher or lower. When choosing the direction of the difference, the reward is a one-tailed test of statistical significance. What this means is that the ability to reject the null is boosted or heightened. The ability to reject the null is called *power*—power to reject the null.

Factors Contributing to Power

There are certain conditions where it is easier to reject the null hypothesis:

- *If using parametric statistics:* Parametric statistics are sort of the elite statistics. Some discussed in this book include the t-test, ANOVAs, and correlational procedures. They are classified as parametric statistics because they make assumptions about population parameters. They work best if the distribution is not skewed but rather a normal curve, bell shaped, and symmetrical. The groups that are compared should have equal variances or spread. This is called *homogeneity of variance*.

    Parametric statistics are more powerful in rejecting the null hypothesis. Also, they are described as *robust*, a statistical term which means that they can hold up even when the assumptions are violated. Parametric statistics rely on the computation of means and standard deviations which use interval and ratio scaling.

    Nonparametric statistics are classified as such because they require meeting very few assumptions. They do not require normal distributions or equal variances. They are oftentimes based on ordinal or nominal measurement and are easier to compute. They use frequency counts instead of complicated calculations. Because nonparametric statistics do not always rely on means and standard deviations, they lack the precision that the parametric statistics possess.

Generally speaking, if the data come from a population that is normally distributed, use the parametric test. If not, use the nonparametric test. In a later chapter, chi-square analysis, an essential nonparametric statistic for use by graduate students, will be discussed.

- *If using a directional hypothesis:* One-tailed tests (used with directional null hypotheses) are more powerful than two-tailed tests (used with nondirectional hypotheses).
- *If using large samples:* These are more powerful than small sample sizes.
- *If using a more liberal significance level:* If choosing .05 instead of .01, the chances to reject the null are greater.

Steps in Hypothesis Testing

The following four steps constitute the basis for hypothesis testing. This framework may be more conceptual since computer programs have taken some of the work out of the steps. Yet it is risky for graduate students to use high-powered statistical packages with very little understanding of the processes involved. Familiarity and awareness are essential for conducting any inferential statistical procedure. This book is based on that premise and will present the inferential statistics in that spirit in the next few chapters that discuss statistical techniques.

1. *State the hypothesis in the null form.* The null can be stated for either differences or relationships. If for differences, the null is either nondirectional or directional, but awareness of the type is a prerequisite.
2. *Select your significance level,* either .05 ($p \leq .05$) or .01 ($p \leq .01$). A significance level of .05 establishes a 95% confidence level and is more liberal but may result in a Type 1 error. A significance level of .01 establishes a 99% confidence level and is more conservative but may result in a Type II error.
3. *Conduct the statistical analysis and obtain the* p *value from the statistical procedure.* Compare the p value to the significance level you chose to determine whether there is a statistically significant result. The *p value* obtained must be less than or equal to the significance level you set in Step 2. If you chose $p \leq .05$, the p value obtained must be .05 or less.
4. *Accept or reject the null.*
   No statistically significant result: accept the null as true.
   Yes, a statistically significant result: reject the null as false.

5. *Determine the practical value of the results.* A result that is statistically significant may be too small to have any value in a real-world setting. If your mean difference is miniscule but statistically significant, what is the practical value? Don't let ego overtake common sense. You have to make a judgment call about your results, and an honest one at that. An objective way to test the practical significance is by using an effect size index like Cohen's d where a small effect size is <.20, a medium effect size is .20 to .79, and a large effect size is >.79. Determining the practical value of your results is an important last step.

A final thought is in order regarding statistical significance. Many are led to believe that getting a statistically significant result is the gold ring. This is not always the case. It depends on what research question is being asked. For example, if the question is whether males and females have different attitudes toward science, it would be positive if there were no significant differences. In this case, a statistically significant result may be meaningful, but not desirable.

Chapter Summary

The use of inferential statistics allows graduate students to make sound conclusions based on data. There is no guesswork. However, a method to the madness must be observed. There is a scientific nature to hypothesis testing: its principles must be respected. But it is a small price to pay for the increase in knowledge that we get in exchange.

CHAPTER EIGHT

t-Test Procedures

For graduate students, many decisions are focused on comparisons such as the following examples:

- To determine which method of instruction has a greater impact on student performance;
- To compare online and print advertisements and their impact on customer purchasing;
- To assess hospital satisfaction between inpatients and outpatients;
- To assess leadership skills before and after manager training; or,
- To evaluate which treatment is more effective in reducing teen substance abuse.

When two groups are compared, the statistic that is most useful is the t-test. It is both an inferential and a parametric statistic.

The purpose of a t-test is to determine if there is a statistically significant difference between the mean scores of two groups. This is where the mean, the queen of central tendency, is vital. The mean scores of two groups are compared via the formula for a t-test. Because the t-test is a parametric statistic, it is powerful. If there are differences, even slight ones, the t-test will uncover them. There are a few basic facts about t-tests:

1. A t-test is used if there are only two groups or two testing times (pre/post or before/after) to compare.

2. This statistical technique answers the null hypothesis: there is no difference between two groups or testing times on respective mean scores.
3. There is one independent variable with two (2) categories and there is one dependent variable.

Independent and Dependent Variables

For many graduate students, there is much confusion around what constitutes independent and dependent variables. To understand the difference is fundamental to executing statistics properly. This is where the use of a statistical software package can be dangerous if you are not aware of even the basic content presented in this book. The simplicity of "click, click" superficially erases the need to know. But understanding which variable is the dependent and which one is the independent variable is vital to producing correct statistical analysis.

The independent variable is independent of the outcome but presumed to cause, affect, or influence the outcome. The dependent variable is dependent on the independent variable; the outcome depends on how the independent variable is used. An independent variable might be patient status (inpatient and outpatient) and the dependent variable might be attitudes toward nursing care. You might administer a survey to determine whether there are different attitudes.

Basically, the *independent variable* for a t-test is nominally scaled. There are two categories with one variable. It is that simple. Many think that because there are two categories, there are two independent variables. There is only *one* independent variable with a t-test, and it has two categories. Table 8.1 presents a few examples of independent variables and their two categories.

Table 8.1. Independent Variables and Two Possible Categories

Independent Variable	1st Category	2nd Category
College students	4-year	2-year
Employees	C-suite managers	Middle managers
Musicians	String	Woodwind
Customers	First time	Repeat
Patients	Maternity	Emergency care
Latinos	Puerto Ricans	Latin Americans
Educators	Teachers	Paraprofessionals
Community	Full-time residents	Summer-only residents

To nominally scale these independent variables for statistical analysis in a t-test, you can assign a "1" to one group and a "2" to the other. Remember, with nominal variables the numbers are only labels. They mean nothing in terms of measurement but everything in differentiating the categories of your independent variable.

With a t-test there is also only one dependent variable. It is continuous in its numeric range and uses ordinal, interval, or ratio measurement scales. Common examples of dependent variables are test scores, health measures, success rates, satisfaction levels, organizational climate, attitudes, and many others. See table 8.2 for some dependent variables that correspond to the independent variables mentioned previously.

Table 8.2. Dependent Variables and Independent Variables

Independent Variable	Dependent Variable
College students	Grade point averages
Employees	Job satisfaction
Musicians	Age
Customers	Dollars spent
Patients	Nurse empathy
Latinos	Political orientation
Educators	Educational level
Community	Attitude toward local schools

Preliminary Assumptions

In the last chapter parametric statistics were described. This group of statistics is more powerful than nonparametric statistics in rejecting the null hypothesis. But they depend on your meeting a few assumptions before you use them. Since the t-test is a parametric statistic, there are a few preliminary steps that you must try to abide by before you implement this statistical procedure:

- *The two groups should have equal variances on the dependent variable.* The variability of the individual groups' mean scores should be equivalent. They should have the same degree of variability. This is called a *test of homogeneity of variance* and done as a preliminary step, a kind of insurance program for your data. This is particularly true when your groups are of different sizes (n)—common in real-world settings versus laboratory settings. The test of homogeneity of variances will be done for you with statistical program packages like SPSS, as a preliminary step for conducting the t-test.

- *The two groups should have an equal number of subjects.* If the two groups are unequal—like 20% more subjects in one group than in the other—look at the standard deviation. If they are similar, go ahead and use the t-test. If it is not, use the Mann-Whitney U test, a nonparametric counterpart, discussed at the end of this chapter.
- *Groups should be equivalent on all other variables except the dependent variables.* If you are examining training approaches in two leadership development programs by comparing scores on a leadership test, make sure that the two groups are similar on other characteristics. These might include gender breakdown, years working at the company, position in the company, educational levels, age, and other variables. These factors could account for the differences and not the leadership development programs.

In your effort to meet the assumptions of the t-test, keep in mind that t-tests are robust. They can hold up even when the assumptions are violated. Although this robustness lets us off the hook to some extent, it is a good idea to approximate to the greatest extent possible the rules of the game, the assumptions. This will ensure excellent data management, avoid errors, and ultimately produce sound data. As a note, many graduate research data sets do not meet these assumptions. The operative word is to *try* to meet them. Your thesis or dissertation is a learning opportunity as a researcher. If your data set violates these assumptions, do not quit. Acknowledge the shortcomings and proceed.

Steps for Conducting a *t*-Test

This example will help to explain the basic purpose of the t-test. Even though there are software programs to click on for a t-test, you should be aware of the process so that you can ensure quality control over the results.

You are a department head of a school with 30 math teachers. Your Kindergarten through eighth-grade (K–8) teachers and those teaching ninth through twelfth (9–12) grades were compared on an instrument used to assess teachers' content knowledge in math. You wondered if there was a difference between the two groups. You decide to compare the math scores between the two groups of teachers.

1. *State your null hypothesis. It is nondirectional.*
   There is no difference in mathematics knowledge between K–8 and 9–12 teachers.

2. *Identify your independent variable and your dependent variable.*

    "Teacher group" was your independent variable with two categories: K–8 teachers and 9–12 teachers. You took the listing of all of your teachers and separated them into two groups. Group One was the K–8 group and Group Two was the 9–12 group. Using nominal scaling, you assign each group a numeric label so that your t-test could be calculated. You used "1" and "2" as your numeric values, which represented the two categories of teachers.

    Your dependent variable was mathematics knowledge, as measured by the score on the math test. You listed the score for each teacher on the mathematics test. You also calculated the mean scores for each of the two groups. The mean scores appeared different, but you could not really tell just from eyeballing the data. A t-test formula had to be applied to the data to determine whether there was a statistically significant difference.

3. *Set up your data for data entry into a database.*

    The data for your t-test was recorded in a statistics database such as that in table 8.3. As a note, you used only the numeric values in your database, that is, the teachers' ID number (1 through 30), the Group codes (1 or 2), and the mathematics test score for each of the 30 teachers. You have data on fifteen K–8 and fifteen 9–12 teachers.

4. *Execute the t-test statistical procedure to obtain a calculated t-value and a probability level.*

    After you have entered your data from your database into the computer software program, you execute the t-test procedure. The statistic obtained is called your *calculated t-value*. The t-value is a continuous number usually with two decimal places. For the sample data, your calculated t-value actually is –4.97. It is critical to your decision whether to reject of accept the null hypothesis.

5. *Examine the p-value on the computer output that is associated with your calculated t value.*

    Is it higher or lower than the significance level you established a priori?

6. *Accept or reject the null hypothesis.*

    Your calculated t-value and its probability level was statistically significant at the significance level you set, $p \leq .05$. You reject the null hypothesis. *There is a difference in mathematics knowledge between K–8 and 9–12 teachers.* You found that your 9–12 teachers had statistically higher mathematics scores.

Table 8.3. Data Set for Two Groups of Teachers and Their Mathematics Scores

ID	Teachers	Category	Group	Math
1	Mr. Ramirez	9–12	1	88
2	Ms. DeJohn	9–12	1	89
3	Ms. Santos	9–12	1	88
4	Ms. Considine	9–12	1	89
5	Ms. Ponte	9–12	1	76
6	Ms. Marchand	9–12	1	89
7	Mr. Ross	9–12	1	88
8	Ms. Beyer	9–12	1	89
9	Ms. Gallagher	9–12	1	88
10	Ms. Magistrali	9–12	1	89
11	Ms. Strand	9–12	1	89
12	Mr. Fischer	9–12	1	88
13	Ms. Bowen	9–12	1	89
14	Ms. Peak	9–12	1	88
15	Mrs. Pacheco	9–12	1	89
	Mean for Group 1			87.73
16	Ms. French	K–8	2	89
17	Mr. Dickinson	K–8	2	78
18	Ms. Addazio	K–8	2	75
19	Ms. Saidel	K–8	2	78
20	Mr. Dwyer	K–8	2	79
21	Ms. Latavia	K–8	2	89
22	Ms. Matarese	K–8	2	78
23	Ms. Kozlak	K–8	2	75
24	Mr. Fitz	K–8	2	78
25	Ms. Hernandez	K–8	2	79
26	Mr. Guzman	K–8	2	78
27	Ms. Santo	K–8	2	75
28	Ms. Strawson	K–8	2	78
29	Ms. Vega	K–8	2	79
30	Ms. Hebert	K–8	2	70
	Mean for Group 2			78.53

Independent and Correlated *t*-Tests

Although this book is intended to keep things as simple as possible, there is a critical addendum to the t-test discussion. There are two forms of the t-test: one is called the *Independent samples* t-test and the other is called the *Correlated samples* t-test, also referred to as a *Paired, Matched, or Dependent Samples* t-test. As graduate students, you need to know whether you are conducting an Independent or Correlated samples t-test.

The Independent samples t-test is quite simple to understand and identify. The two groups, such as the K–8 and 9–12 teacher groups, have *no relationship* to each other. They are independent of one another, hence the name "Independent samples" t-test.

Conversely, Correlated samples t-tests use two groups that have a connection or relationship to each other. With this built-in relationship, it is more likely that the mean scores of the two groups have a relationship too. So, the Correlated samples formula takes the inherent relationship into account and helps to find a statistical significance—if there indeed is one. Here are the occasions when you might be using Correlated t-tests:

1. *When you are measuring the same individual twice*
   Two groups of data are really the same individual with two scores on them. Table 8.4 displays an example where the patients in a weight loss program are measured twice on weight pre- and postprogram. For each patient, the pair, or dual weights, compose the two groups of data needed for a t-test.

   Table 8.4. Patients and Their Pre- and Postweight

	Preweight	Postweight
Olivia	120	110
Joey	120	120
Luke	130	125
Mia	150	145

   Correlated t-tests are used most often for this purpose—if you want to determine impact, efficacy, and persistence over time. Some examples of when a correlated t-test might be used include the following:
   - When assessing the efficacy of a health care intervention, treatment, or drug over two time periods
   - When tracking community involvement from last year to this year
   - When monitoring the effect of professional development training on knowledge acquisition, pre and post

2. *If you have matched your sample on some other variable so that the two groups are alike.*
   One of the primary tenets of the t-test is that the two groups you are studying are alike *except* for your dependent variable. You want to ensure that something else called *extraneous variance* or error does not

account for differences between the two groups instead of your dependent variable.

For example, look at the data set of teachers, discussed previously. What might account for the difference in mathematics knowledge besides whether a teacher is K–8 or 9–12? The answers might be the years in teaching, the amount of professional development, confidence with the subject area, attitude toward the profession, or other factors. If there was one particular factor that you felt might compromise your data, you might try to match the groups on that variable so that they are equivalent except for the dependent variable you were exploring.

Matched Samples

Here is an example of a matched sample. Using the same set of data that we used in the t-test, the two teacher groups were matched on the number of professional development courses they had taken. As you can see in table 8.5, each teacher in Group One is matched with another teacher in Group Two on the number of professional development courses that they took. For each ID number in Group One there is a member of Group Two that has the exact same number of professional development courses. Ramirez with French, DeJohn with Dickinson, and all the way through, there are pairs of teachers with the same number of professional development courses in each of the two groups.

Table 8.5. Teachers Matched on Professional Development (PD) for the Correlated *t*-Test

Pair	9–12 Teachers	PD	Group	Math	K–8 Teachers	PD	Group	Math
1	Mr. Ramirez	1	1	88	Ms. French	1	2	89
2	Ms. DeJohn	1	1	89	Mr. Dickinson	1	2	78
3	Ms. Santos	2	1	88	Ms. Addazio	2	2	75
4	Ms. Considine	3	1	89	Ms. Saidel	3	2	78
5	Mr. Ponte	4	1	70	Mr. Dwyer	4	2	79
6	Ms. Marchand	1	1	89	Ms. Latavia	1	2	89
7	Mr. Ross	4	1	88	Ms. Matarese	4	2	78
8	Ms. Beyer	5	1	89	Ms. Kozlak	5	2	75
9	Ms. Gallagher	3	1	88	Mr. Fitz	3	2	78
10	Ms. Magistrali	4	1	89	Ms. Hernandez	4	2	79
11	Ms. Strand	5	1	89	Ms. Guzman	5	2	78
12	Mr. Fischer	1	1	88	Ms. Santo	1	2	75
13	Ms. Bowen	2	1	89	Ms. Strawson	2	2	78
14	Ms. Peak	2	1	88	Ms. Vega	2	2	79
15	Ms. Pacheco	3	1	89	Ms. Hebert	3	2	70

The number of professional development courses would not be entered into the t-test that you were calculating, but it would ensure that your groups of teachers were equivalent on this important variable (number of professional development courses) before you begin to compare mathematics knowledge. Your null hypothesis is still focused on grade levels and on mathematics knowledge, not the number of professional development courses.

Degrees of Freedom

Independent sample and Correlated sample t-tests have different *degrees of freedom* associated with each t-test form. *Degrees of freedom* are noted in professional journals as *df*. You need to know how the degrees of freedom are attained so that you can report your statistical results.

- If you use an Independent samples t-test, the degrees of freedom (*df*) are equal to the number in your total sample minus 2 or [N – 2]. In the first example of K–8 and 9–12 teachers, the degrees of freedom would be 28 [or 30 teachers – 2 = 28].
- If you are using a Correlated samples t-test, the degrees of freedom (*df*) are equal to the number of pairs minus 1 [N of pairs – 1]. In the second example of teachers, you used matched pairs on professional development courses; the degrees of freedom would be 14 [or 15 pairs – 1].

Correlated samples t-tests make it more difficult for you to reject the null. Since the data for the groups are related, you have to ensure that the difference you find is real and not due to the relationship between the sets of data. Therefore, the bar is raised with Correlated t-tests in the computation for statistical significance with respective degrees of freedom and critical cutoff points for rejecting the null. (Statistical textbooks will have a deep discussion of degrees of freedom along with statistical computations of t-tests for graduate students who are interested.)

Reporting *t*-Test Results in a Table Format

This is how you might report your t-test findings in a table format. For an *Independent samples* t-test, there are two groups of teachers with 15 (*N*) in each group. The two mean scores on the math test and the respective standard deviations are reported. The t-value that is calculated with the SPSS statistical package is 4.97, there are 28 degrees of freedom, and the calculated *p-value* is .00. This is below the cut off level of significance you chose, which was .05. You have statistically significant results; the null is rejected (see table 8.6).

Table 8.6. Reporting Independent Samples *t*-Test Results

Teacher Groups	N	M	(SD)	t value	df	p
9–12 teachers	15	87.33	(4.82)	4.97	28	.00*
K–8 teachers	15	78.53	(4.87)			

*$p \leq .05$

This is how you might report your t-test findings in a table format. For a *Correlated samples t*-test, there are 25 workshop participants tested twice, pre and post. The two mean scores on a leadership test and the respective standard deviations are reported. The t-value that is calculated with the SPSS statistical package is 4.69, there are 24 degrees of freedom, and the calculated *p-value* is .00. This is below the cut off level of significance you chose, which was .05. You have statistically significant results; the null is rejected (see table 8.7).

Table 8.7. Reporting Correlated Samples t-Test Results

N = 25	M	(SD)	t value	df	p
Preworkshop	84.72	(6.07)	4.69	24	.00*
Postworkshop	90.56	(3.72)			

*$p \leq .05$

Nonparametric Counterparts

There are two nonparametric statistical procedures that answer the same question that the t-test does. If the assumptions mentioned in the beginning of this chapter are violated, then you may want to consider using a nonparametric alternative. The Mann-Whitney U test and the Wilcoxon matched-pairs signed ranks test are the counterparts to the Independent and Correlated samples t-tests, respectively. They are not bound by normal distributions or equal variances. They can be used with ordinal data or ranked data instead of interval/ratio scaling for the dependent measure. These nonparametric counterparts can be executed in a statistical program like SPSS. The downside is that they are not as powerful as the parametric t-tests in rejecting the null hypothesis.

Chapter Summary

T-tests are very useful tools. Often, you are comparing two groups of students, managers, patients, employees, customers and so forth. The t-test is a simple and straightforward statistic that allows you to get beyond a frequency count. One group's mean score may look different from another's mean score, or it may look the same. The litmus test for *statistically significant* two group comparisons is called the t-test.

CHAPTER NINE

ANOVA Procedures

The t-test is very useful when you have two groups or testing times (pre/post or before/after) to compare. But what happens if you have more than two? The statistical technique that is analogous to the t-test is called *Analysis of Variance* or ANOVA. The purpose of ANOVA is understood quickly if it is thought of as an extension of the t-test.

ANOVA is an inferential statistic. It is also a parametric statistic and as such it is very powerful. It can reject the null hypothesis or find differences if they exist among groups. The assumptions of homogeneity of variance, equal group sizes, and normal distribution of scores should be adhered to, just as the t-test should meet these assumptions. Yet as a robust statistic, ANOVA can sustain having the assumptions violated and still perform its function. There is a nonparametric version of ANOVA called the Kruskal-Wallis H test. If you have serious violations of the assumptions, use it.

ANOVA is a little more complicated than a t-test even when using a statistical software package. Although there are many versions of ANOVA (which will be described briefly), this book will focus on a simple version, One-Way ANOVA. For the purpose of discussion, the main point is that you use ANOVA as you would a t-test but *when there are more than two groups*. There is one dependent and one independent variable but with more than two levels or categories.

Here are some facts about One-Way ANOVAs:

- This statistical technique answers the null hypothesis: there is *no difference* among three or more (3+) groups on their respective mean scores.
- There is one independent variable with three or more (3+) categories. These levels are nominally scaled. As a note, you can use an ANOVA to compare two groups, but the t-test is intended for that purpose.
- There is one dependent variable. It is continuous in its numeric range and uses ordinal, interval, or ratio measurement scales, similar to the t-test.
- The statistic you obtain to determine statistical significance is the *F ratio* or F statistic.

Steps for Conducting a One-Way ANOVA

An example will help to explain the basic purpose of the One-Way ANOVA. You want to explore tobacco usage among teens in three towns that have different demographic profiles (urban, suburban, and rural). You think that there might be differences among the three towns, and such information would be helpful for public health messaging and town planning.

1. *State your null hypothesis.*
   There is no difference in tobacco usage among teens in three towns.
2. *Identify your independent variable and your dependent variable.*
   "Town of residency" is your independent variable with three categories: Town A, Town B, and Town C. Using nominal scaling, you assign a numeric label so that your ANOVA can be calculated. You use 1, 2, and 3 as your numeric values, which represent the three towns. Your dependent variable is number of cigarettes smoked for a one-month period by each teen. You have also calculated the mean number of cigarettes for each group of teens by town. The number appears different, but you cannot really tell until an ANOVA procedure is applied to the data.
3. *Set up your data for data entry into a database.*
   The data for your One-Way ANOVA might be recorded in a database that looks like table 9.1. There are three sets of teens with a total of 39 teens altogether (*N*). The groups are not exactly the same size, but close enough not to seriously violate assumptions of equal group size. The *Town Code* and the *Number of cigarettes smoked* by each teen are the only pieces of data that are entered into your statistical formula or statistical package.

Table 9.1. One Way ANOVA Data Set: Town of Residency and Cigarettes Smoked for a Month

Teen		Town	Town Code	Cigarettes Smoked
1.	Traci	Town A	1	123
2.	Karen	Town A	1	119
3.	Betsy	Town A	1	120
4.	Maria	Town A	1	103
5.	Jose	Town A	1	168
6.	Jesus	Town A	1	190
7.	Angel	Town A	1	120
8.	Margaret	Town A	1	130
9.	Bonita	Town A	1	103
10.	Ernest	Town A	1	104
11.	Miguel	Town A	1	189
12.	Sherri	Town A	1	100
	Town 1 $(n = 12)$			**Cigarettes Smoked** $M = 131$
13.	Kathy	Town B	2	120
14.	Giovanna	Town B	2	190
15.	Ginger	Town B	2	189
16.	Kim	Town B	2	145
17.	Ernesto	Town B	2	171
18.	Lucia	Town B	2	189
19.	Anna	Town B	2	145
20.	Eric	Town B	2	177
21.	Juan	Town B	2	189
22.	Pedro	Town B	2	167
23.	Angela	Town B	2	156
24.	Abdul	Town B	2	189
	Town 2 $(n = 12)$			**Cigarettes Smoked** $M = 169$
25.	Pepe	Town C	3	120
26.	Maureen	Town C	3	134
27.	Marci	Town C	3	155
28.	Peter	Town C	3	134
29.	Paulo	Town C	3	144
30.	Annie	Town C	3	133
31.	Rebecca	Town C	3	142
32.	Alisha	Town C	3	123
33.	Steve	Town C	3	110
34.	Irving	Town C	3	102
35.	Micah	Town C	3	130
36.	Nina	Town C	3	190
37.	Dana	Town C	3	100
38.	Guillermo	Town C	3	103
39.	Francesca	Town C	3	120
	Town 3 $(n = 15)$			**Cigarettes Smoked** $M = 129$

4. *Execute the ANOVA statistical procedure to obtain an F ratio, the calculated value, and a probability level.*

    After you have entered your data from your database, you can execute the ANOVA. The *F ratio* is the statistic in ANOVA that indicates if you can reject the null. Parallel to the t-test procedure, the *F ratio* is called your calculated value. It is usually a three- to four-digit number with two decimal places. For our data set the calculated *F ratio* is 8.94.

5. *Examine the p-value on the computer output that is associated with the calculated F ratio.*

    Is it higher or lower than the significance level you established a priori? The traditional significance levels are .05 or .01. You have selected a significance level of $p < .05$. The actual *p*-value is .00.

6. *Accept or reject the null hypothesis.*

    Your calculated value was statistically significant at the probability level you set, $p \leq .05$. You reject the null hypothesis. *There is a difference in tobacco usage among teens in the three towns.*

7. *Conduct follow-up tests (called post hoc tests) to determine where the differences lay.*

Post Hoc Tests

When you have statistical differences with t-tests, there are only two mean scores. You can look to see which is higher and which is lower and then draw your conclusions and inferences. If you have a statistically significant result with ANOVA, your work is not complete. The only answer you have obtained at this point is that there *are* statistically significant differences among your groups: in this example the teens from the three towns. But which towns are different on the variable of tobacco usage? Several possibilities for significant differences might exist:

- *Between teens in Town A and Town B (A and B)*
- *Between teens in Town A and Town C (A and C)*
- *Between teens in Town B and Town C (B and C)*

With ANOVA there are more than two mean scores. You cannot eyeball the means to see which is higher and then make deductions. You have to conduct an additional statistical procedure. A follow-up test, called a *post hoc* procedure or a multiple comparison test, is designed just for this purpose. It shows exactly where the significant differences lay after (post) a *significant*

F ratio is obtained in ANOVA. It pinpoints which mean scores are significantly different from each other.

There are many options of *post hoc* procedures to choose from. Each is named after the data scientist who developed it.

- Fisher's LSD
- Duncan's new multiple range test
- Newman-Keuls
- Tukey's HSD
- Scheffé test

Some are more conservative than others are, making it harder to reject the null. A liberal procedure will find a significant difference between two mean scores that are relatively close together. A conservative procedure will indicate that two mean scores are significantly different only when the means are far apart. The Fisher LSD is the most liberal and the Scheffé test, the most conservative of the post hoc tests.

You may wonder why t-tests are not used to compare each of the combinations above. That would be logical except for the fact that conducting multiple t-tests increases the chances of getting spurious results with error. As the number of t-tests increase, the probability of getting a statistically significant difference by chance alone also increases. This means you are approaching Type I error territory. Post hoc or multiple comparison tests adjust the level of significance to reduce the influence of error.

For the Town example, you conducted a Scheffé multiple comparison test. It showed that the level of cigarette-smoking in Town B was significantly different from that in both Town A and Town C on number of cigarettes smoked per month. However, the levels for Town A and Town C were not different from each other. Textbox 9.1 shows how you might report your findings in table format. There are other ways to report ANOVA findings that can be found in professional journals in different formats.

Degrees of Freedom with ANOVA

When you set up a table for One-Way ANOVA results, you must report the degrees of freedom associated with the ANOVA procedure. The degrees of freedom for ANOVA procedures are a bit more complicated and can cause some confusion. There are two numbers that compose your degrees of freedom for ANOVA: the Between Groups degrees of freedom (*df*) and the Within Groups degrees of freedom (*df*).

Textbox 9.1. One-Way ANOVA Table: Town of Residency and Cigarettes Smoked per Month

Town of Residency	M	(SD)	F ratio	df	p
Town A	130.75	(32.92)	8.94	2,36	.00*
Town B	168.92	(23.03)			
Town C	129.33	(23.39)			
Total	141.95	(31.64)			

*$p \leq .05$

(Scheffé post hoc: Town B is significantly different from both Town A and Town C. There is a significantly higher number of cigarettes smoked by teens in that town compared to the other two towns.)

- The Between Groups *df* is equal to the number of groups minus one. In this case you had three towns. Your Between Groups *df* is 2 or (three groups – 1).
- The Within Groups *df* is equal to the number in each group minus one, and then the sum for each group. In your case the Within Groups *df* is 36. It is calculated like this:
Group 1 [12 – 1] = 11 +
Group 2 [12 – 1] = 11 +
Group 3 [15 – 1] = 14+ = 36

For the ANOVA example, the degrees of freedom are these two numbers: 2 and 36. You will see it often reported like this (*df* = 2, 36) with a comma separating the *between* from the *within*.

Other Versions of ANOVA

There are other versions of ANOVA procedures besides One-Way Analysis of Variance. These become more complex because of the added variables or factors in the research designs. There are multiple F ratios, interaction effects, and other aspects that make the following procedures more sophisticated both to execute and to interpret. Here are some basics on each, but you may need help in executing and interpreting these research designs and corresponding statistics.

Factorial ANOVAs

Two-Way ANOVA

ANOVA designs, called *factorial ANOVAs*, compare *more* than one independent variable. Let's use the same example that we had in One-Way ANOVA, but add another independent variable, also referred to as a "factor." Besides town of residency, we will add school (middle or secondary). This design is called a Two-Way ANOVA.

Now we have *Town* of residency as one independent variable, and *School* as a second independent variable. Instead of three groups that we had in One-Way ANOVA, we have six groups because of the two independent variables. Sometimes, a design such as this would be listed as a 3 × 2 design. This means there are two independent variables: one with three categories and one with two categories. Each of the six groups' mean scores (M) on your one dependent variable of "Number of Cigarettes Smoked" will be compared by the *Two-Way ANOVA* (see table 9.2).

Table 9.2. 3 × 2 ANOVA Design: Town of Residency by School

Town A	Town B	Town C
Middle	Middle	Middle
M	M	M
Town A	Town B	Town C
Secondary	Secondary	Secondary
M	M	M

Three-Way ANOVA

This can further become a *Three-Way ANOVA* by adding yet another independent variable or third factor. Let's add "coffee usage." There are now three independent variables with twelve separate groups on which the dependent variable (M) will be measured. The three independent variables will have three categories (Town), two categories (School), and two categories (coffee usage). This may be called a 3 × 2 × 2 ANOVA design (see table 9.3).

Table 9.3. 3 × 2 × 2 ANOVA Design: Town of Residency by School by Coffee Usage

Town A Middle Coffee M	Town B Middle Coffee M	Town C Middle Coffee M
Town A Secondary Coffee M	Town B Secondary Coffee M	Town C Secondary Coffee M
Town A Middle No coffee M	Town B Middle No coffee M	Town C Middle No coffee M
Town A Secondary No coffee M	Town B Secondary No coffee M	Town C Secondary No coffee M

Analysis of Covariance: ANCOVA

There is another very useful statistical procedure called *Analysis of Covariance* or ANCOVA. One purpose of this technique is oftentimes used to make groups equivalent before they are compared on the dependent variable.

As you may recall, one of the primary rules of the t-test, as well as ANOVA procedures, is that the groups you are studying are alike *except* for your dependent variable. You want to ensure that something else (called extraneous variance or error) does not account for differences between or among the groups. ANCOVA adjusts for differences so that the focus of the analysis is the dependent variable and not error.

As an example, your graduate research study is on the impact of leadership training on managers at corporate versus nonprofit settings When both groups of managers are tested on their leadership skills with a leadership questionnaire, the *pretest* results (before any training occurs) show statistically significant differences in mean scores between the two groups. ANCOVA is used to statistically equate the two groups' pretest scores on leadership before the training is implemented. This allows you to determine whether a real difference occurred over time at posttesting.

ANCOVA determines if the training produced different results in leadership skills, when the program is concluded, by equating the mean differences found at initial (pre) testing. The differences at pretesting could be due to age, college degree, and other factors that make the groups nonequivalent before the leadership training is undertaken. The pretest results on the leadership questionnaire are made equivalent so the posttest results on the leadership questionnaire can be reliable comparisons of training efficacy.

Repeated Measures ANOVA

There are occasions when we need to measure something on a recurrent basis. You measure the dependent variable more than once; you repeatedly measure it. This is where the statistical procedure gets its name, *Repeated Measures ANOVA*.

For example, your research might conduct employee satisfaction measurements in September, again in January, and once again in September a year later to track improvement in job satisfaction over time. Or you measure patient response to a pharmaceutical drug intended to reduce cholesterol levels at multiple times. All of these occasions might lend themselves to using a Repeated Measures ANOVA procedure to determine changes over time and to track results. Repeated measurements are needed to do that. This statistical procedure allows for repeated testing on the dependent variable.

Chapter Summary

One-Way ANOVA is a very useful statistic and a great partner to the t-test. It functions quite the same but affords us the opportunity to expand the number of groups beyond two. This is often called for in many settings where more than two categories exist for graduate student research. The conceptual steps to One-Way ANOVA follow the t-test with the exception of the need to conduct post hoc tests after significant results are obtained. Many statistical packages like SPSS offer this option as part of One-Way ANOVA.

For statistical questions that are more complex (in that they add more variables to the research design), there are statistical models to accommodate them. Factorial ANOVA, ANCOVA, and Repeated Measures ANOVA are sophisticated statistical procedures that have been described in the most elementary fashion here. Reference to statistical or mathematical textbooks will present a more detailed discussion for interested graduate students.

CHAPTER TEN

Chi-Square Procedures

In the previous two chapters we discussed parametric statistics that answer questions about differences between groups (t-tests) and among groups (ANOVAs). Parametric statistics are of great value and used often. Yet one of the most valuable and popular statistics is a nonparametric procedure called *chi-square*. It is also called the test of "goodness of fit." Its symbol is X^2.

Unlike the t-test and ANOVA procedures, chi-square is not as powerful to reject the null. It does not use the mean or standard deviation for computation; it does not rely on an interval or ratio scaling. Because chi-square relies on categorical data, its value lays in the statistic's ability to answer questions about data that are nominal and/or ordinal. Variables are measured very often by their categories and not exact intervals. So, chi-square allows you to answer important questions with variables measured with nominal or ordinal scales. This is of great value to graduate student research in many theses and dissertations.

Steps for Conducting a Chi-Square Analysis

An example of a chi-square analysis will promote the merit of this statistical technique. Your graduate research is examining different levels of technological proficiency in new hires at your company. During the past year the company hired 40 (n) business majors and 40 (n) engineering majors, or 80 (N) new hires in all.

1. *State your null hypothesis.*
   There is no difference between business and engineering hires on technological proficiency. (This null hypothesis sounds similar to the hypotheses for t-tests and ANOVAs. However, chi-square is used because it allows us to forgo many assumptions needed for t-tests and ANOVAs, and it relies on nominal and ordinal scaling.)
2. *Identify your two categorical variables.*
   The first is *major* field of study with two categories:
   - Business
   - Engineering

   The second is technological *proficiency* with four categories:
   - Novice
   - Apprentice
   - Practitioner
   - Expert
3. *Set up your data for data entry into a database.*
   Table 10.1 is the data set that indicates the *major* field of study and the technological *proficiency* for your 80 new hires.

   You have decided to code *major*:
   - Business (1)
   - Engineering (2)

   Technological *proficiency* has been coded:
   - Novice (1)
   - Apprentice (2)
   - Practitioner (3)
   - Expert (4)

   For data entry, you will only use numeric data as in table 10.1.
4. *Set up a contingency table of your expected frequencies.*
   (As a note, you do not have to do this because statistical programs will do this for you in the analysis. But it is good to understand how the chi-square analysis operates.)

   A contingency table of *expected* frequencies is an arrangement of your categorical data into a two-way classification scheme. One of the classifications becomes *rows* (across) and the other becomes *columns* (down). The boxes, formed by the intersection of rows and columns, are called *cells*. The cells tell us *what you can expect*, given the frequencies of rows and columns. It is a simple application of probabilities based on your sample numbers and their classifications. Table 10.2 displays a contingency table of *expected* frequencies for your data.

Table 10.1. Data Set for Eighty New Hires by Major Field of Study and Technological Proficiency

ID #	Major	Proficiency	ID #	Major	Proficiency
1.	1	2	41.	2	2
2.	1	2	42.	2	2
3.	1	2	43.	2	2
4.	1	2	44.	2	2
5.	1	2	45.	2	2
6.	1	2	46.	2	2
7.	1	2	47.	2	2
8.	1	2	48.	2	2
9.	1	2	49.	2	2
10.	1	2	50.	2	2
11.	1	1	51.	2	4
12.	1	1	52.	2	4
13.	1	1	53.	2	4
14.	1	1	54.	2	4
15.	1	1	55.	2	4
16.	1	1	56.	2	4
17.	1	1	57.	2	4
18.	1	1	58.	2	4
19.	1	1	59.	2	4
20.	1	1	60.	2	4
21.	1	3	61.	2	4
22.	1	3	62.	2	4
23.	1	3	63.	2	4
24.	1	3	64.	2	4
25.	1	3	65.	2	4
26.	1	3	66.	2	4
27.	1	3	67.	2	4
28.	1	3	68.	2	4
29.	1	3	69.	2	4
30.	1	3	70.	2	4
31.	1	3	71.	2	1
32.	1	3	72.	2	1
33.	1	3	73.	2	1
34.	1	3	74.	2	1
35.	1	3	75.	2	1
36.	1	3	76.	2	1
37.	1	3	77.	2	1
38.	1	3	78.	2	1
39.	1	3	79.	2	1
40.	1	3	80.	2	1

Table 10.2. Contingency Table of *Expected* Frequencies

	Business	Engineering	Row Total
Novice	10 (25%) Cell	10 (25%) Cell	20 (25%)
Apprentice	10 (25%) Cell	10 (25%) Cell	20 (25%)
Practitioner	10 (25%) Cell	10 (25%) Cell	20 (25%)
Expert	10 (25%) Cell	10 (25%) Cell	20 (25%)
Column Total	40 (50%) Cell	40 (50%) Cell	N = 80

In the case of this example, the columns (down) correspond to *Major* field with *two* categories. You allocate two columns for each of the two major field categories. The rows (across) correspond to the variable of technological *Proficiency* and have *four* different categories. You allocate four rows for each of the four levels. You have 80 new hires altogether.

The classification for "columns" creates *two* categories of major field. Since there are 80 new hires, 50% are expected to be business ($n = 40$) and 50% are expected to be engineering ($n = 40$). The "rows" for technological proficiency break into *four* categories. Since there are 80 new hires, 25% are expected to be Novice ($n = 20$), 25% are expected to be Apprentice ($n = 20$), 25% are expected to be Practitioner ($n = 20$), and 25% are expected to be Expert ($n = 20$).

Next you have to calculate the cells. The expected frequency of any cell in the table is found by multiplying the total n of the column with the total n of the row to which the cell belongs. The product is divided by the total sample size (N). To obtain a cell for Business, you multiple the total of the column (40) times the total of the row (20) and divide by 80, the sample size. You get 10 as your cell size. This is your expected frequency for each cell. It is helpful to report the cell size as well as its percentage. In table 10.2, Expected Frequencies has both.

You have just constructed a contingency table of *expected* frequencies from the two nominal variables for your 80 new hires. Each cell has 10 new hires in it because of the breakdown of the two classification variables: *major* field and technological *proficiency*. What you would *expect* for your new hires as outcomes is that ten engineering and ten business *majors* will populate each of the four rubric *proficiency* classifications if there were no differences between the two major fields on technological proficiency. The contingency table of *expected* frequencies enables you to determine the nature of the relationships between your two categorical variables.

5. *Execute the chi-square statistical procedure to obtain a calculated value and probability level.*

   The chi-square analysis produces a contingency table of *actual* frequencies from the actual frequency data from your new hires. It looks like table 10.3.

Table 10.3. Contingency Table of *Actual* Frequencies

	Business	Engineering	Row Classification
Novice	10 (25%)	10 (25%)	20 (25%)
Apprentice	10 (25%)	10 (25%)	20 (25%)
Practitioner	20 (50%)	0 (0%)	20 (25%)
Expert	0 (0%)	20 (50%)	20 (25%)
Column Classification	40 (50%)	40 (50%)	N = 80

It also produces a chi-square statistic of 40.00. This is called your *calculated value*. The degrees of freedom (*df*) for a chi-square statistic are calculated by taking the [number of rows − 1 × the number of columns − 1]. In the case of your new hires, you have two rows (major field) and four columns (technological proficiency). The degrees of freedom equals [2 − 1 × 4 − 1] or 3.

6. *Examine the p-value on the computer output that is associated with the chi-square statistic.*

   Your calculated value for chi-square is 40.00 with three degrees of freedom. Your calculated value was statistically significant at the probability level you set, $p \leq .05$. The *expected* frequencies were significantly different from what you observed to be true in your *actual* frequencies.

7. *Accept or reject the null hypothesis.*

   You reject the null hypothesis. There is a difference between business and engineering new hires on technological proficiency. The engineering majors had more technological proficiency than did business majors.

Reporting Chi-Square Results

From the study of new hires, major fields of study, and technological proficiency levels, here is a simple format for reporting chi-square results. The degrees of freedom (3), the number of subjects (80), the chi-square statistic

(40.00), and the significance level (.00) are reported. The results can be as simple in a narrative like this. X^2 (3, $N = 80$) = 40.00, $p \leq .05$. Or you can develop a table of results that looks like table 10.4 or table 10.5.

Table 10.4. Reporting the Chi-Square (X^2) Results with Expected and Actual Frequencies

New Hires N = 80	Frequency	Novice	Apprentice	Practitioner	Expert	X^2 $df = 3$
Business	Expected	10 (25%)	10 (25%)	10 (25%)	10 (25%)	40.00*
40 = n	Actual	10 (25%)	10 (25%)	20 (50%)	0 (00%)	
Engineering	Expected	10 (25%)	10 (25%)	10 (25%)	10 (25%)	
40 = n	Actual	10 (25%)	10 (25%)	0 (00%)	20 (50%)	

* $p \leq .05$

Table 10.5. Reporting the Chi-Square (X^2) Results with Actual Frequencies Only

New Hires N = 80	Novice	Apprentice	Practitioner	Expert	X^2	df	p
Business (n = 40)	10 (25%)	10 (25%)	20 (50%)	0 (00%)	40.00	3	.00*
Engineering (n = 40)	10 (25%)	10 (25%)	0 (00%)	20 (50%)			

* $p \leq .05$

Collapsing Categories to Make Cells Larger

Sometimes when chi-square analyses are used, the cell sizes are small. This is problematic for the statistic to operate optimally. As a recommendation, have at least five values in each cell. What should be done if this shortcoming exists in the data? Collapse the smaller cells to create larger cells. It must be done with caution, and it must make sense.

For example, the US Census Bureau's coding contains over 30 Hispanic or Latino subgroups. The major ones are Mexican, Cuban, and Puerto Rican. There are a few other subgroups like Salvadoran or Nicaraguan. If there were too few numbers in these two categories, it would make sense to combine Salvadoran and Nicaraguan into one group to give the subgroup more values for statistical analysis. You might call this combined group of two "Central American Latinos," for example.

Other Nonparametric Statistics

There are other statistical procedures for use with nominal and ordinal scaled data. Statistics texts will go into more detail about them but here are a few that graduate students might be interested in using:

- The *Fisher's exact test:* This test is used to compare two independent samples with respect to a dichotomous variable. This is similar to the chi-square test just described, but the Fisher's exact test works better when there are few subjects in the data set. If that is a limitation, this is the statistic that helps with a solution.
- The *Mann Whitney U test:* This statistic is used to compare groups by using rankings on variables of interest. Both groups are independent just as with the Independent samples t-tests. This statistic does not use mean scores but rather ranking of data to determine differences.
- The *Kruskal-Wallis H test:* This test is an extension of the Mann Whitney U test but used with three or more groups, parallel to the one-way ANOVA procedure. It uses a similar methodology to the Mann Whitney U Test with rankings.
- The *Wilcoxon-matched pairs signed-ranks test:* Similar to the correlated t-test, this statistic uses data where there is repeated measurement. If the data are ordinal or the assumptions of the t-test cannot be met, this statistic is useful.

The *sign test*, the *binomial test*, and the *median test* are among other nonparametric procedures that are useful to consider. Again, they are less powerful than their parametric counterparts to reject the null hypothesis. This means a Type 2 error has more likelihood of occurring. Certainly, they should be considered as part of the array of strategies that graduate students can avail themselves of, if the situation calls for alternatives.

Chapter Summary

The chi-square statistic, which relies on nominal and ordinal scaling described in chapter 1, is used very often because graduate research has categorical variables. The chi-square statistical procedure allows us to compare groups against each other on important variables. Although it may not have the sophistication of its parametric counterparts, its utility may exceed theirs. It is a statistical technique that provides us with insights that would be impossible to diagnose if you had to depend on statistics that required interval or ratio scaling.

CHAPTER ELEVEN

~

Correlation Procedures

Besides focusing on differences, graduate research focuses on *relationships*. There are times when we wonder if two factors are linked. For example, we may ask some of the following questions:

- Does the amount of coffee consumption in the evening relate to the ability to fall asleep?
- Does the incidence of juvenile delinquency vary with the age of a teen?
- Does on-screen time by children impact their verbal communication skills?
- Does exposure to behavioral therapy help with body weight reduction?
- Does job performance correlate with absenteeism?
- Is patient compliance related to hospital readmission?
- Does daily writing in student journals increase reading comprehension?
- Can leadership skill development impact the opportunities for advancement?

There are statistics that help to determine if relationships do exist, and if so, what are the characteristics of those relationships? This is where correlations are useful statistical techniques. They test the extent to which two variables occur together, and how related they are. As statistics, correlations can be descriptive and inferential at the same time. They can describe your data and can also infer relationships from samples to populations.

What Data Are Needed for Correlations?

You need two sets of variables (or paired observations) on the same individuals. In correlations, the first variable is called x. The second variable is called y. Your data are paired observations of x and y on one subject. You correlate x and y to see if there is a relationship. For the purpose of illustration, let's say that we wanted to know if physical fitness and weight were related for corporate executives. We thought if you were physically fit, you would weigh less. If you were in poor shape, you would weigh more. Fitness and weight would be our two variables for our paired observations. We would collect our data on all of our corporate executives. For each, we would have Weight (x) in pounds and a Fitness (y) score. Then we would calculate a correlation statistic and find the answer.

There are basically four questions that correlational procedures can address. Each is followed by an example of variables that you might correlate with each other:

1. If one variable [x] *increases* does the other variable [y] *increase*?
    Example: Greater parent-to-child reading time increases school readiness.
2. If one variable [x] *decreases* does the other variable [y] *decrease*?
    Example: The less time patients spend out of bed, the less their mobility.
3. If one variable [x] *increases* does the other variable [y] *decrease*?
    Example: Increased sports participation by teens decreases cell phone usage.
4. If one variable [x] *decreases* does the other variable [y] *increase*?
    Example: Employee satisfaction declines when overtime requirements increase.

Correlation Coefficients (r)

The relationship between two variables, and the nature of that relationship, is measured by *a correlation coefficient*, symbolized by the letter r. A correlation coefficient is a two-digit decimal such as −.20 or +.78. The numerical values can range from minus one (−1.00) through zero (0) to plus one (+1.00). However, −1.00 and +1.00 are perfect correlations; you rarely see these numbers in the real world. (You can find numeric formulas for computing correlation coefficients in any statistical text.)

Strength and Direction of the Correlation

The correlation coefficient is a great statistic because a single number summarizes the *strength* and the *direction* of the relationship between two variables. This is a lot of information.

Strength

The actual numeric value of the correlation coefficient tells us the *strength* of the relationship. The nearer the number is to either +1.00 or −1.00, the stronger the relationship is between the two variables. Correlations of −.88 and +.88 have the same strength. A correlation of −.88 is stronger than a correlation of +.87 by only an infinitesimal amount.

A zero correlation ($r = 0$) indicates absolutely no correlation whatsoever. The relationship between the amount of rainfall and an employee's salary would have no correlation ($r = 0$). Correlations of −.07 or +.02 are negligible. Although there is no hard and firm interpretation of what constitutes strength of all correlation coefficients, here are some suggestions of strength.

Table 11.1. Strength of Correlation Coefficients

Correlation Coefficient	Strength of the Correlation
0	No correlation
±.01 to ±.30	Negligible to low
±.31 to ±.50	Low to moderate
±.51 to ±.70	Moderate to high
±.71 to ±.99	High to extremely high
±1.00	Perfect correlation

Correlations and Shared Variance

As a note, a correlation coefficient should not be interpreted as a percentage. Since it is a decimal, this can happen, but is incorrect. If the correlation between salary and level of employee turnover is .50, you cannot conclude that salary accounts for 50% of turnover. You must square the correlation coefficient and multiply it by 100 to assess the shared variance of two variables. This is called a *coefficient of determination* (noted by r^2). For this example, 25% (r^2) is the shared variance between the two variables of salary and turnover. You can conclude that 25% of turnover can be explained by salary. This coefficient of determination (r^2) is the percentage of variance held in common by the two variables. Table 11.2 indicates the correlation coefficients and the percentage of shared variance. As you can see, you must have an extremely high correlation to assume that two variables are part of each other.

Table 11.2. Correlation Coefficients and Coefficient of Determination

Correlation Coefficient (r)	Coefficient of Determination (r^2)
.10	1%
.15	2%
.25	6%
.50	25%
.75	56%
.80	64%
.85	72%
.90	81%
.95	90%
.98	96%

Direction

Relationships between two variables can either be positive or negative. That is what is meant by *direction*. Therefore, correlation coefficients can be either positive or negative. A plus or a minus sign before the numeric value indicates direction.

If a correlation is positive, it means that

- if one variable (*x*) increases, the other (*y*) increases, or
- if one variable decreases (*x*), the other (*y*) decreases.

Positive correlations sometimes have a plus sign before the decimal, but many times it is implied. A positive correlation of +.67 might also look like .67.

If a correlation is negative, it means that

- if one variable (*x*) increases, the other (*y*) decreases, *or*
- if one variable (*x*) decreases, the other (*y*) increases.

There is always a minus sign before the correlation to indicate a negative correlation. These are also called *inverse* correlations.

Steps for Conducting a Correlation Statistical Technique

The following example will demonstrate the qualities of asking questions with correlational statistics. Let's say that you have 20 preteens in your community who are at risk for dropping out of school. You believe that those who participate in after-school clubs and extracurricular activities have better attendance in school.

1. *State your null hypothesis.*
   There is no relationship between school attendance and participation in extracurricular activities.
2. *Identify your two variables, x and y.*
   Your variable "x" is the total number of days in attendance, as tabulated at the end of the school year. The variable "y" is the total number of after-school and extracurricular activities the child participated in during the school year.
3. *Set up your data for data entry into a database.*
   Table 11.3 displays the data set for the preteens and the two variables: attendance (x) and extracurricular activities (y).
4. *Execute the correlation statistical procedure to obtain a calculated value, the correlation coefficient (r).*

Table 11.3. Data Set for Attendance (X) and Extracurricular Activities (Y)

Preteens	Attendance Out of 180 Possible Days	Number of Extracurricular Activities
1. Emmy	140	1
2. Auggie	170	7
3. Lowen	150	2
4. Elise	135	2
5. Mila	160	5
6. Luna	175	8
7. Mackie	160	6
8. Catrina	155	3
9. Jose	165	8
10. Juan	135	2
11. Wes	180	8
12. Rosalyn	165	7
13. Felicity	145	3
14. Mark	140	3
15. Miguel	155	3
16. Craig	145	1
17. Oliver	175	8
18. Alex	180	7
19. Rebecca	170	7
20. Seth	175	9

There are different correlation techniques that will be discussed shortly and are available in statistical software programs. For these data, you have selected a Pearson product moment correlation coefficient. The correlation coefficient calculated is +.92 (r). From the plus sign (+) and the size of the correlation coefficient (.92), you can see that there is a strong, positive correlation between attendance and extracurricular activities for preteens.

1. *Examine the computer output to compare the p value that is associated with the correlation coefficient.*
   The degrees of freedom for a Pearson product moment correlation coefficient is (the number of pairs − 2). In this case there were twenty pairs of data with the two variables so the degrees of freedom was 20 minus 2, or 18. As calculated, your actual p value for the data was .00 and your level of significance was $p \leq .05$.
2. *Accept or reject the null hypothesis.*
   You reject the null hypothesis. There is a significant relationship between after-school/extracurricular activities and school attendance. The direction and strength tell you that as one variable increases, so does the other. Specifically, participation in extracurricular activities boosts school attendance for preteens at risk for dropping out. Furthermore, the shared variance (r^2) is 84%—the correlation coefficient squared. This means that 84% of school attendance can be explained by the number of extracurricular activities a preteen in this community is involved in.

Sample Size and Significance of Correlation Coefficients

The likelihood of obtaining a statistically significant correlation coefficient is based on sample size. If you have a large sample, you often have a statistically significant correlation coefficient. For example, you can have ninety-two pairs of data and at the .05 level of statistical significance ($df = 90$) and a correlation of $r = .22$ would be statistically significant. However, this is a low correlation when strength is considered. The *strength* of the correlation coefficient is much more important than its statistical significance. Graduate students need to recognize this very important fact. Those who are less informed would use statistical significance to make their case, and it would be deceiving due to sample size alone. Look at the strength (size) of the correlation coefficient and pay less attention to the p value.

Reporting Correlation Results
Reporting a correlation coefficient is very simple. Just use r and the equal sign. For example, the previous example would be reported like this:

$$r\,(20) = +.92, p = .00$$

The number in parentheses is the number of subjects, 20. The correlation statistic follows and then the *p value* for statistical significance. For our data set, we would report in the narrative that there was a strong correlation between extracurricular activities and school attendance. You may want to show your actual data set. A scattergram for illustration would highlight the impact that one variable had upon the other. What is a scattergram?

Scattergram, Also Called a Scatterplot

As we learned with frequency distributions, graphing techniques can illustrate a statistical message quickly and clearly. Similar to a frequency polygon, the *scattergram* is a graphic representation of your correlation data. (Many software programs can generate these for you.) You start with the vertical (ordinate) and horizontal (abscissa) axes on a graph. For your data set, you place the "number of extracurricular activities" on the vertical axis starting with 1 and ending with 10, a little above the highest value in your data set. On the horizontal axis is the total number of days in attendance in the school year using intervals of 10 days. Then, you plot variables *x* and *y* for each preteen on your graph. Place a dot on the graph where the two variables intersect. Our scattergram looks like figure 11.1.

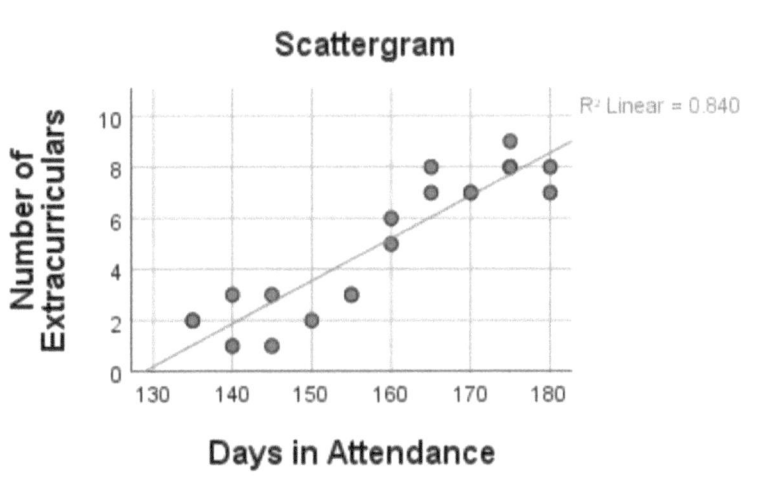

Figure 11.1. Scattergram for Attendance and Extracurriculars. Source: *Author developed*

Scattergrams are very useful because they tell us a lot about our two variables and their relationship. Here are the pieces of information that scattergrams supply.

1. *Scattergrams can tell the strength of the relationship between the two variables.*
   - If the dots cluster close to an imaginary line, there is a very strong relationship or correlation between the two variables.
   - When the dots are scattered in an ellipse or cigar-shape, there is a moderate correlation.
   - When the dots are scattered randomly around the graph, there is a low or negligible correlation.

   The scattergram in figure 11.1 shows the dots clustering close to an imaginary line or the line penciled in on the scatter diagram. This illustrates a very strong relationship between the two variables. The tighter the clustering of dots, the stronger the relationship. In the case of our data set, the number of extracurricular activities might be considered a predictor of school attendance. The dots are clustered into a fairly tight line.

2. *Scattergrams can tell the direction of the relationship between the two variables.*
   - If the slope of the line falls from left to right, there is a negative correlation.
   - If the slope of the line rises from left to right, there is a positive correlation.

   The latter is the case with the data in our scattergram. The slope of the line rises from left to right signifying a positive correlation. The slope of the line indicates that as extracurricular activities increase, so does school attendance. Conversely, a positive relationship *also* means that as after-school and extracurricular activities decrease, so does attendance. Just looking at the slope tells us a great deal about the relationship between these two variables.

3. *Scattergrams can also show outlier scores.*

   Values completely out of range with all the others should be considered for elimination in the calculation of a correlation coefficient. They might contaminate the data set and give misleading results if a correlation coefficient is calculated. In our example, there are no outlier scores. All of our *x/y* intersections fall close to the line. But look at figure 11.2, which has some outliers in it.

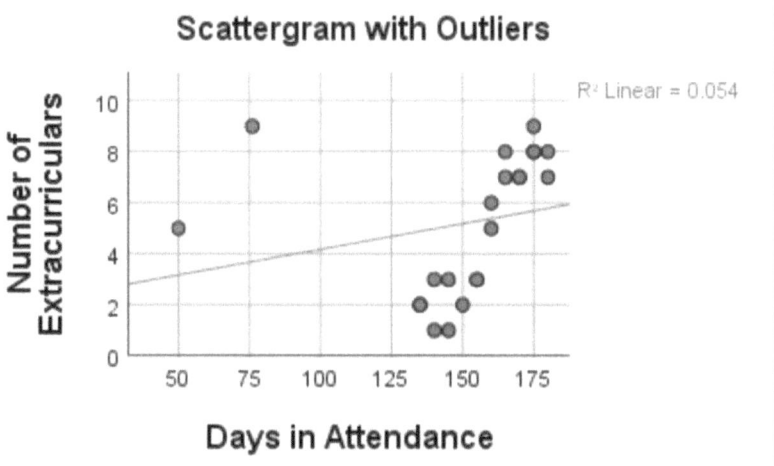

Figure 11.2. Scattergram for Attendance and Extracurriculars with Outliers. *Source: Author developed*

Practical Application of Correlations

There are many uses for correlations that you can avail yourselves of.

1. The most useful purpose is to see if two variables are correlated. This is what chapter 11 has focused on.
2. Another important function of the correlation procedure is with respect to tests or instruments we measure with. The *reliability* of a test is reported as a correlation coefficient. It measures whether the test consistently measures what it purports to measure. You can be confident of that when you examine the correlation coefficient, reported in the test manual as the "reliability coefficient." If it is $r = .80$ or $r = .75$, we can be certain that it is a pretty reliable measurement tool. Medical instruments have high reliability coefficients; personality tests or vocational interest assessments would have lower reliability coefficients.
3. A third function is performed by correlational statistics. If you are interested in determining whether two raters or two observers are seeing the same thing when they collect information, you are looking for *inter-rater reliability*. For example, if two of your managers were evaluating the customer service for the same group of bank tellers, you would want their observations (recorded by a checklist or rubric) to be very similar. By correlating their data, you would create an inter-rater reliability coefficient. Hopefully, the correlational numeric value would be strong.

Types of Correlation Techniques

- *Pearson product moment correlation* is a parametric statistic and requires interval or ratio data on both the x and the y variables to calculate it. This is the premier correlation statistic. As a parametric statistic, the assumptions of homogeneity of variance and normal distribution apply—just as they do with t-tests and ANOVAs. Pearson product moment correlation is called Pearson r.
- *Point biserial procedure* is a nonparametric statistic and uses a dichotomous, nominal-scaled variable and an interval/ratio scaled variable to calculate it. An example might be correlating tardiness (late/on time) *and* frequency of behavioral problems at work.
- *Spearman's Rho* is a nonparametric statistic that uses ordinal-scaled data with ordinal-scaled data for computation. It correlates two sets of ranks to determine their degree of equivalence. An example might be the relationship between customer satisfaction levels *and* their agreement with restaurant policy on wearing beach attire in the dining area.
- *Rank biserial* is a nonparametric statistic and uses a dichotomous, nominal-scaled variable and an ordinal-scaled variable to calculate it. An example is language spoken in the home (Spanish/English) *and* satisfaction with communication from the hospital emergency department.
- *Phi coefficient* is a nonparametric statistic and correlates two dichotomous, nominally scaled variables. An example might be the relationship between college type (public/ private) *and* STEM major field of study (yes/no).

Chapter Summary

There is one last and very important point to make when correlations are discussed. No attempt should be made to say that one variable (x) *causes* the other variable (y). This is untrue. A correlation only suggests that a relationship exists between the variables. It does not mean that one variable causes the other. The use of correlational statistics is a great asset. It suggests that relationships exist. To use them to pinpoint causality is a misuse of a highly valuable statistical technique.

CHAPTER TWELVE

Regression Procedures

This chapter is a brief and basic discussion of multiple regression. It is largely a conceptual presentation of a complex statistic. Textbooks will provide more depth for graduate students interested in this statistical procedure. As a note, there are entire graduate level courses called Multiple Regression.

Correlation and linear regression are sometimes thought of as one and the same. There are similarities but they are different. Correlation attempts to determine if a relationship exists between two variables. Regression has two distinctive purposes:

- *Explanation:* A variable, sometimes more than one, is used to *explain* another variable of interest. Nurses' satisfaction with the profession might be *explained* by salary, hours, hospital resources, patient mix, supplies, or building maintenance.
- *Prediction:* A variable, sometimes more than one, is used to *predict* another variable of interest. Student tardiness might be *predicted* by access to transportation, parental support, attitude toward school, or food security.

Another difference is the labeling of the variables. The variables that explain or predict are the independent variables. The variable that is explained or predicted is the dependent variable. In the previous *explanation* example, the independent variables are salary, hours, hospital resources, patient mix, supplies, and building maintenance. The dependent variable is nurse satisfaction.

In the previous *prediction* example, the independent variables are access to transportation, parental support, attitude toward school, and food security; and the dependent variable is tardiness.

The several points you should consider before conducting a linear regression procedure are:

- Independent variables should have a moderate to strong relationship (correlation) with the dependent variable. If they are going to be used to predict or explain the dependent variable, it is common sense that they should have a strong relationship with it.
- Independent variables should not have a moderate to strong relationship (correlation) with each other. If the predictors are highly correlated with each other, they will overlap or explain the same variance in the dependent variable. They will be redundant and not useful for either explanation or prediction.
- Variables should be quantitative, continuous variables. Ordinal, interval, or ratio scaling are advised. (If categorical or nominal scaled variables are used as predictors, they need to be dummy coded in a special manner. It would be advisable to get statistical advice on how to do this because it is not a matter of just entering nominal codes.)
- Variances of the dependent variable should be similar across all levels of the independent variable. This is called *homoscedasticity* in regression. (This is similar to the assumption in ANOVA and t-tests called homogeneity of variance.)

Bivariate or Simple Regression

The most basic type of regression is called bivariate or simple regression. As with simple correlation, there are only two variables that give the regression model its name. In this regression procedure the independent variable is used to explain or predict the dependent variable.

As an example, a high school math teacher felt that midterm grades could explain attitudes toward math. She has the data on her 2022 freshmen students that contain two variables: their actual fall midterm grades and their attitude toward math scores. She conducts a bivariate multiple regression procedure. The regression produces a statistic called a Multiple R (R). With just two variables, the bivariate regression Multiple R looks just like the Pearson correlation coefficient (r). The difference is that with regression, the purpose is explanation and not just description. If a scattergram were constructed, dots intersecting the two variables (attitude toward math and midterm exam grade) would form an ellipse, approximating a straight line. The independent variable would show its effectiveness in explaining the dependent variable. This line is called the *regression line* or *line of best fit*.

The Coefficient of Determination (R^2)
In order to tell if the regression model is strong, the *coefficient of determination* (R^2) is examined, just as it is with the correlation coefficient discussed in the last chapter. The R^2 measures the proportion of dependent variable that is explained by the independent variable. If the R^2 was .04, only 4% of the variance in the dependent variable (attitude toward math) was explained by the independent variable, midterm grade (not much). If the R^2 was .84, 84% of the variance in the dependent variable (attitude toward math) was explained by the midterm grade (a great deal).

The Regression Equation
The bivariate regression procedure is very useful because it provides elements for building an equation. This equation can be used in predicting the dependent variable with *subsequent sets* of sample data. Regression procedures have been used by college admissions officers to predict who should be admitted to their institutions. It is used in weather forecasting to predict hurricane seasons. It is used for many events for which data are known to predict the unknown future.

Continuing with the high school math teacher example, the bivariate regression output with the 2022 freshmen student data produced a coefficient of determination R^2 of .75, very strong. It looks like the regression 2022 data could be useful in predicting attitudes of her 2023 class of freshmen. She decides to use the regression procedure statistics from last year's freshmen class (2022) *to predict attitudes of this year's freshmen class (2023)*. Here is how she does this.

On the bivariate multiple regression output from 2022 there are elements that provide for building a regression equation. The equation looks like this:

$$\hat{Y} = a + b \text{ times } X$$

The variable $\hat{Y}$ is the *unknown* dependent variable being predicted: the attitude toward math. The variable X is the *known* independent variable, the actual midterm grade for the 2023 students. The bivariate regression statistical output that the teacher used with the 2022 class data provides the number for the a (the constant) and b (the regression coefficient or slope). (As graduate students you need to know where to find *a* and *b* on the computer output like SPSS.)

For each student in her 2023 class, the math teacher uses the equation by putting in the value for *a* (the constant), the value for *b*, and the freshman's actual 2023 midterm grade (X) to predict their attitude toward math ($\hat{Y}$). The equation is calculated like this: you add the value for *a* with *b* times the midterm grade (X) and you get a predicted score on attitude toward math ($\hat{Y}$). The equation is below.

$$\hat{Y} \text{ (attitude toward math)} = a + b \times X \text{ (midterm grade)}$$

The teacher can now identify those freshmen whose attitudes are predicted to be negative, and then provide support as they begin the second half of their freshmen year of high school. The bivariate regression equation developed from the 2022 class of freshmen will help to identify those 2023 freshmen whose attitude toward math may be low.

Multiple Regression: Correlating More than Two Variables

Many research settings are multivariate environments. This means that more than one factor usually accounts for what is happening. So how do graduate students address this fact? Multiple regression procedures help with this. As with any statistical software program, a click of the mouse produces statistical output, but it is not always correctly executed. Multiple regression may be an area where more statistical expertise is required so that your findings are reliable and valid.

Like bivariate regression, multiple regression has one dependent variable ($\hat{Y}$). Also, there are the same reasons for its use, explanation, and prediction. Another similarity is that a regression equation is produced. Lastly, both are inferential statistics, which look to the independent variables to account for the variance in the dependent variable. The key difference is that there is more than one independent variable (X).

The multiple regression equation with one dependent variable ($\hat{Y}$) and two independent variables looks like this:

$$\hat{Y} = a + b_1 \times (X_1) + b_2 \times (X_2)$$

(X_1) and (X_2) are the two independent variables. There is always a constant (*a*). There is a regression coefficient or slope (*b*) for each independent variable (X).

There could be a third independent variable and the equation would look similar. There is always one constant (*a*). There is a regression coefficient *or slope* (*b*) for each independent variable (X).

$$\hat{Y} = a + b_1 \times (X_1) + b_2 \times (X_2) + b_3 \times (X_3)$$

The introduction of multiple independent variables is intended to assess the extent to which each can explain or predict the dependent variable. Previous assumptions are worth repeating:

- Independent variables must have a strong relationship with the dependent variable.
- Independent variables should have a low correlation with each other.

Some Commonly Used Forms of Multiple Regression
Here are three forms of multiple regression procedures that graduate students might use:

- *Simultaneous multiple regression* enters the independent variables all at once into the procedure to see if they together can explain the variance in the dependent variable. This is like a stew where all meats and vegetables are thrown into the pot together at once. There is no order to the entry of independent variables.
- *Stepwise multiple regression* uses a stepwise entry of the independent variables based on their incremental, nonoverlapping ability to explain the dependent variable. This procedure selects out the most efficacious independent variable first that explains the most variance in the dependent variable. Then, it selects the next independent variable that explains any variance that is left. And on with the next independent variable until the incremental variance explained by predictors is exhausted.
- *Hierarchical multiple regression* has a controlled entry of the independent variables based on a predetermined plan. For this procedure there is a deliberate method designed by whomever is executing the regression procedure. For example, when exploring what factors might predict college selectivity, average household income of a town might be entered first, as a controlling variable. Here it is acknowledged that household income of the town likely explains much variance in college selectivity. However, variables such as high school rank, number of AP credits, or size of school might also be considered important factors for their effect

on college selectivity. Conducting the regression procedure this way allows the variance from income to be extracted first or controlled, but then allows the other variables the chance to explain or predict the college selectivity.

Steps for Conducting Multiple Regression

The following example will demonstrate the process of using a multiple regression procedure. A department manager wants to explore what influences organizational climate among the 77 employees in the department. The perception is that organizational climate is explained by two factors: job satisfaction (measured by a total score on a survey) *and* the years employed. The department manager has employee scores on an instrument measuring organizational climate as well.

1. *State the null hypotheses.* Organizational climate ($\hat{Y}$) is not explained by a combination of job satisfaction (X_1) and years employed (X_2).
2. *Identify the multiple regression variables.* The dependent variable is organizational climate ($\hat{Y}$) and the two independent variables are job satisfaction (X_1) and years employed (X_2).
3. *Set up the data for data entry* into a statistical software database. There are data on 77 employees with numeric values on organizational climate ($\hat{Y}$), job satisfaction (X_1), and years employed (X_2) in the database.
4. *Execute descriptive and correlational statistics* to examine the data before running the multiple regression procedure.

These statistics are provided in statistical packages like SPSS as part of the regression procedure. Table 12.1 displays the descriptive statistics on the three variables under study. The means (M) and standard deviation (SD) are produced for each variable X_1, X_2, and $\hat{Y}$.

Table 12.1. Descriptive Statistics for the Multiple Regression

Variables	N	M	SD
Organizational climate ($\hat{Y}$)	77	79.94	14.25
Job satisfaction (X_1)	77	78.79	13.27
Years employed (X_2)	77	17.01	8.83

Table 12.2 produces the correlations among the three variables. This is an important piece of information. It indicates that the independent variables

are correlated with the dependent variable to differing degrees, and the independent variables have a low correlation with each other. That is what is desired when a multiple regression procedure is used.

Table 12.2. Correlation Matrix of Variables in the Multiple Regression

	Organizational Climate ($\hat{Y}$) r	Job Satisfaction (X_1) r	Years Employed (X_2) r
Organizational climate ($\hat{Y}$)	1.00	.88	.40
Job satisfaction (X_1)	.88	1.00	.37
Years employed (X_2)	.40	.37	1.00

5. *Execute a simultaneous multiple regression procedure* where the two independent variables of job satisfaction (X_1) and years employed (X_2) will attempt to explain organizational climate ($\hat{Y}$).
6. *Examine the p value that is produced on the summary table for multiple regression.*
   Statistical packages like SPSS provide many pieces of statistical information in the summary table like that in table 12.3. Look carefully for these: Multiple R, R^2, F ratio, degrees of freedom, and *p value*.

Table 12.3. Partial Summary Table for Multiple Regression

R	R^2	F	df1	df2	p
.88	.78	127.30	2	74	.00*

*$p \leq .05$

For this example, a Multiple R of .88 was obtained. This is a very strong correlation, but more importantly the R^2 or coefficient of determination was .78. This indicates that 78% of the variation in organizational climate was explained by job satisfaction and years employed. The F ratio was 127.30 with 2 and 74 degrees of freedom. The *p value* was .00. The statistical significance of the regression procedure is reported like this: R = .88, F (2,74) = 127.30, $p \leq .05$.

7. *Accept or reject the null hypothesis.* Organizational climate ($\hat{Y}$) is explained by a combination of both job satisfaction (X_1) and years employed (X_2). The null is rejected. However, were each of the two independent variables similarly successful in explaining the variance?
   One way to assess this is by using a t-test, which the multiple regression procedure provides as part of the SPSS statistical output. The first t-test value for job satisfaction (X_1) is 14.21 with a probability value of

.00. It is lower than the significance level of $p \leq .05$ and is a statistically significant independent variable. However, the second T-test value for years employed (X_2) is 1.50 with a probability value of .14, not statistically significant. This independent variable did not add much to the explanation of organizational climate, the dependent variable ($\hat{Y}$). It was largely explained by job satisfaction (X_1).

8. *Set up scattergrams to display the findings from the multiple regression.* The *line of best fit* in figure 12.1 shows that there is a strong relationship between job satisfaction (X_1) and organizational climate ($\hat{Y}$). The dots that intersect the two variables create a linear picture, forming a straight line. The slope rising from left to right tells us of a positive relationship. The scattergram in figure 12.2 for the years employed (X_2) show little relationship to organizational climate ($\hat{Y}$).

If the manager wanted to use these data to monitor organizational climate in the department over time (such as year to year), the regression equation could be generated from data in table 12.4.

$$\hat{Y} = a + b_1 \times (X_1) + b_2 \times (X_2)$$

($\hat{Y}$) = 6.16 (a) + .91 (b_1) × (job satisfaction X_1) + .14 (b_2) × (years empl. X_2)

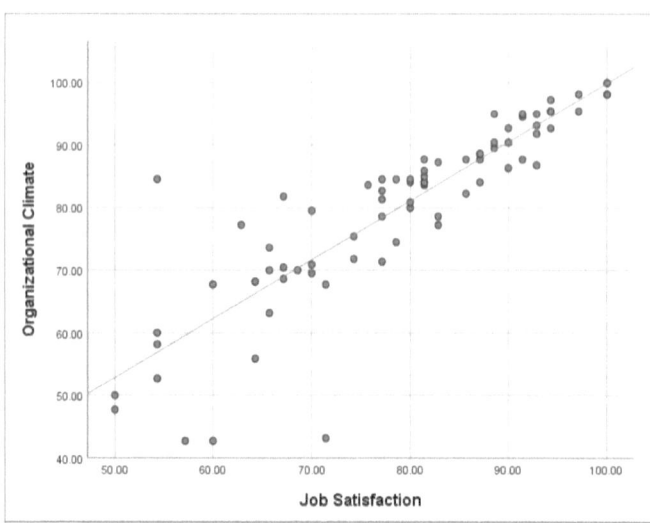

Figure 12.1. Scattergram: Organizational Climate by Job Satisfaction. *Source: Author developed*

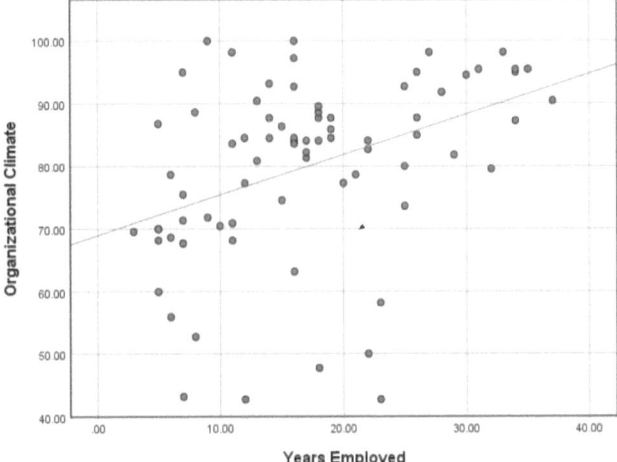

Figure 12.2. Scattergram: Organizational Climate by Years Employed. *Source: Author developed*

Table 12.4. Constant, Regression Coefficients, and t-Tests

	B	t value	p
Constant (a)	6.16		
Job satisfaction (X_1)	.91	14.21	.00*
Years employed (X_2)	.14	1.50	.14

*$p < .01$

Chapter Summary

The occasion to undertake a regression procedure may be commonplace due to the nature of correlated variables in research settings. Given that fact, graduate students should consider using this statistic if the situation warrants. Some expert assistance may be worth the investment, but the insights produced are invaluable. The concepts behind this statistic are fairly straightforward. However, some understanding of this statistic is necessary because a click of the mouse will produce output, but it may be misinformation if done incorrectly.

CHAPTER THIRTEEN

Practical Tips for Graduate Students

Starting the Research Process

Select a general research topic before you dive into the library or the internet and drown in the resources. Go through this brief evaluation before you make a commitment to an area of inquiry. This exercise will reduce your stress and contribute to a topic that you will enjoy and will be acceptable to your degree granting institution. There are several ways that you can determine if your topic is a good one. Here are some strategies that you can use to *assess the value* of your research topic:

- Consider your own interest in the topic. Are you genuinely interested in it and willing to spend days, weeks, months, and maybe even years focused on it? Are you willing to do the work to become an expert on this topic? Is it one you would really enjoy exploring?
- Evaluate the importance of the topic. Is it something that will be of benefit to the field you are part of? Will your work on this topic add to the body of knowledge? Is there some practical value that other professionals in your field can use or apply that makes your topic of actionable value?
- Is your topic relevant and timely? Is it something that others in your field have written about in the recent past? Is it an area of discussion right now, or is it passé? Is there a new treatment that you would like to compare to another one or one that is older? Is there a gap in the body of knowledge that you would like to fill? Are there contradictions in

results published in the literature that you would like to address? Does it build upon someone else's work but has a different twist? Is it an original idea or has it already been done with conclusive results?
- Is the time required to complete the research on this topic realistic? Is the topic something you can research within a timeframe or is the commitment of time too great for you to undertake as a graduate student?
- What is the level of difficulty? Is your topic one that has sensitivity, geography, or complexity that will make the process of investigating it filled with extra stress? Does controversy surround it? Do you have to travel far and wide to access the data sources? Is it so complex that you will drown in the process of doing the research?
- What are the out-of-pocket expenses associated with your topic? Analyze the costs of pursuing it. Is the topic one that fits within a student's limited budget or will the cost exceed the pocketbook?

Use multiple library and online resources to establish keywords to get the ball rolling; add keywords as you move along. "Research the research" in the literature review process. Here are a range of resources that can help you search the literature, thoroughly and efficiently. Remember to add keywords as you go along with the purpose of "researching the research."

- Books (primary and secondary sources)
- Journals (professional association, trade journals, popular magazines)
- Newspapers (*The New York Times, The Wall Street Journal, The Washington Post*)
- Videotapes (your own, documentaries, films)
- Indices: ask a Reference Department librarian for help to find the right ones (*Reader's Guide, Education Index, Index Medicus,* ERIC, and others)
- Federal, state, governmental reports (Census Data, Public Health, Department of Labor, etc.)
- Interviews
- Doctoral dissertations or graduate theses in your own college or university library
- *Dissertation Abstracts*—a librarian can help you find this source
- Websites and blogs

Take your time in the library and online when reviewing the literature. Avoid costly and embarrassing mistakes because you were rushing. It is incredibly easy to make literature review errors when you are first starting out on this task. Listed below are some of the most common ones that graduate students make during their review of the literature. You will see that avoiding them usually requires just a little slowing down, and thoughtful planning on your part. Literature review is oftentimes done in a hurry instead of systematically. Sources are overlooked or skipped because

- you rely on secondary sources and forget the primary sources;
- you read journal article results sections only and not the methodology sections, which give hints to producing good dissertations or theses;
- your topic is too broad; the literature becomes unwieldy and massive;
- you make copies with pages missing;
- you neglect to generate *new* key words as you pursue the literature review; or
- you forget to use the reference section of journal articles to generate lists of more pertinent articles.

Use index cards to take notes and to guide your actual writing. It seems antiquated but you can shuffle the cards. They are physical and can be moved in a different order for easy writing of narratives.

Selecting the Research Design

Research design and methodology are plans that promote systematic management of statistical data collection. Design and methodology dictate what you need to answer your research questions. There are many types of research designs for graduate research. Some are mixed methods, which means that a combination of methods is used—possibly quantitative and qualitative approaches. Here are a few of the basic designs.

Historical Research Design: The purpose is to collect, verify, and synthesize evidence to establish facts that defend or refute your hypothesis. It uses primary and secondary sources and lots of qualitative data sources such as logs, diaries, official records, reports, and other documents. The limitation is that the sources must be both authentic and valid. Hypothetical examples include the evolution of bottle feeding for infants or the evolution of the laptop computer.

Case and Field Research Design: Also called *ethnographic* research, it uses direct observation to give a complete snapshot of a case that is being studied. It is useful when not much is known about a phenomenon. It uses few subjects. Hypothetical examples are the investigation of hospice services on a terminally ill patient or observations of Muslim children in the American classroom.

Descriptive or Survey Research Design: It attempts to describe and explain conditions of the present by using many subjects and questionnaires to fully describe a phenomenon. Survey research design/survey methodology is one of the most popular for graduate research. These can be executed online, by mail, by phone, or administered to intact groups. The latter is the most cost effective and quickest way to collect your data! You don't need an example of a survey in this day and age, but one might be the public's view of American leaders.

Correlational or Prospective Research Design: It attempts to explore relationships and/or to make predictions. It uses one set of subjects with two or more variables for each to examine relationships. This research design might show the relationship between smoking, exercise, and diet on heart health, or maternal exercise during pregnancy and its impact on newborns.

Causal Comparative or Ex Post Facto *Research Design:* This research design attempts to explore cause and effect relationships where causes already exist and cannot be manipulated. It uses what already exists and looks backward to explain why. This research design might look at divorced couples and examine causes by looking back on their relationships while married, or surgical patient recovery and satisfaction with their hospital stay.

Developmental or Time Series Research Design: Data are collected at certain points in time going forward. There is an emphasis on time patterns and longitudinal growth or change. This research might examine the impact of exposure to STEM content in college to see if it positively impacts students' choice of careers, or monthly peer counseling and its impact on juvenile delinquency.

Experimental Research Design: This design is most appropriate in controlled settings such as laboratories. The design assumes *random selection* of subjects and *random assignment* to groups (experimental and control). It attempts to explore cause and effect relationships where causes can be manipulated to produce different kinds of effects. Because of the requirement of random assignment, this design can be difficult to execute in the real-world (nonlaboratory) setting. An example of experimental research is the impact of an experimental antidepressant on patients with one group receiving a placebo. Another example is water with and without fluoride and the effect on dental health.

Quasi-Experimental Research Design: These typically have some of the features of the true experiment such as control groups with a before and after intervention. They are not done in the laboratory setting but in the field that creates a less perfect comparison. However, they may provide more real-world application. An example of this type of design might be the comparison of two sets of business leaders with leadership training for one group and the other with none to determine if corporate metrics were impacted. Another example is two innovative curricula and their impact on third graders' reading abilities.

Writing Your Dissertation or Thesis

You have designed your study, collected data, and analyzed it; you are almost finished at this point. Take the time to end on a high note. Here are some tips in writing your dissertation or thesis.

Use a Standard Organizational Framework to Format the Text

When you begin to write your findings, it is imperative that you address the format. A recommendation is to use a standard organizational framework to format the text. The school you are enrolled in probably has a template for you to follow. Use it. Also, find peers who have done similar dissertations or theses at the school you are enrolled at and look at theirs for guidance. Organization is important for telling your story; for explaining what your graduate research and statistics have uncovered.

You also need to keep your advisors connected to your findings. They need to follow a logical sequence to understand the purpose of the study, the methodology, and how findings were arrived at. A well-constructed narrative will provide the reviewers with all of the necessary information including

- the theoretical rationale for the research;
- the research questions and hypotheses to be answered;
- the design and methodology;
- the subjects and sampling procedures;
- the methods and procedures of data collection;
- the instruments selected to collect data, their reliability, and validity;
- the statistical findings; and
- the implications, limitations, and follow-up research opportunities.

Keep the Text Concise and to the Point

Dissertations and theses do not have to be three inches thick or 500 pages long. Use concise text that is to the point. Some graduate students bury a main finding in so much verbiage that the reader becomes confused or misses it altogether. Sometimes two points are grouped together, also adding to confusion.

As simple as it sounds, make your points one at a time. Keep the text simple, clear, and readable without run-on sentences and extraneous descriptive language. High-sounding language is not impressive and will only diminish the impact of your findings. Make the paragraphs straightforward. Boil it down, and then boil it down again. If the tables are well-conceived, a lot of narrative is unnecessary. Do not add statistical jargon. If it is absolutely essential, make it user friendly by defining it and its purpose. Otherwise, leave it out.

Use Tables to Present and Illustrate Your Findings

Tables can be your best friend in writing the main body—the statistical findings. They should be used to both present and illustrate your statistical findings. Usually, the statistical tables are developed after the statistics are tabulated in SPSS or another software package. This provides you with the means to have the tables to use when you tackle the narrative portion. Writing directly from the tables, generated by the study, will take the guesswork out of organizing the findings. It will be easy to present the findings logically in a way your advisors can follow.

Keep the tables simple. Some tables are intimidating because of the large amounts of numbers they present. It is recommended that only one or two variables be presented in one table. If you are reporting gender and grade levels, that is enough in one table. Instead of putting several variables in one table, use several tables to simplify the presentation.

Do not report numbers without percentages. In your tables that describe categorical variables or those variables with nominal or ordinal scales, do not list the numbers in each category without the corresponding percentages. With raw numbers only, you make the reader work hard; why should they? Again, make the data easy to grasp. Percentages convert raw data in categories into meaningful information. The message is immediate and clear.

Consider Including Graphs If They Add to the Comprehension of the Findings

Many graduate students fill up pages in their dissertations or theses with graphs. There is an abundance of pie charts, histograms, scattergrams, and a host of other pictures cluttering the statistical findings. Consider including graphs if they add to the comprehension of your statistical findings.

The prudent use of frequency polygons, histograms, bar charts, pictographs, pie charts, and scattergrams is strongly urged—if they add to the results of your work. If not, leave them out. Above all, use them if there is an inherent message that is conveyed. Do not add "so what" graphs. If you have a graph, it should stand alone without text narrative or numbers to tell some story. Many times, they do not add anything except color and design. This is not a project in graphic arts; it is a serious research study.

Have Your Dissertation or Thesis Read by an Independent Reviewer
Having your work read by an independent reviewer is an important factor in quality control. This final piece of advice for writing your dissertation or thesis is probably the last thing you will want to hear but it is strongly urged. It is one of the most critical steps in producing the final document. You are tired of this whole process. You have done a lot of work. And you want to be finished. But, as a graduate student, you have been married to this work for months and even years. You may be too familiar with the subject matter or too impressed with your own writing style. As a result, sufficient detail may be lacking in the explanation of some findings or too much abstract language used in others.

Typographical errors leave a bad impression and take away from your credibility. If words are misspelled, or there are grammatical errors, this can only work against you, regardless of the quality of the research you are presenting. Have a colleague, a family member, or friend critically review your work before it goes to the next step. It may save a lot of blood, sweat, and tears. You have climbed the highest mountain and are almost at the top. Don't let this last step be the spoiler.

Chapter Summary

Research is hard work, and it requires a commitment over time. One of the greatest barriers to completing the thesis or doctorate is implementing the research methods, including statistics. This book is intended to help you move through the barriers that seem formidable *but are not*. With a little persistence and time, you can master the research challenge and become the success that you set out to be when you signed on to your academic journey. In the process, you will find that conducting research can be gratifying in so many ways. The content of this book is to help you find joy in that process, and maybe even to continue to do research after your degree is obtained. Good luck.

About the Authors

Susan Rovezzi Carroll is president of Words & Numbers Research, Inc. She received her doctorate in 1981 and served as a faculty member at the University of Connecticut prior to founding the research and evaluation firm in 1984. Her expertise is in research design, instrumentation, and statistical analysis. Dr. Carroll has provided guidance and support to hundreds of graduate students in the United States and abroad. Her website for graduate student support is www.dissertation-statistics.com. Her office email is dr.carroll@optonline.net.

David J. Carroll is vice president of Words & Numbers Research, Inc. He received an MSW in planning and evaluation in 1977. David has expertise in demographic analysis, development of social indicators, and strategic planning. He has conducted comprehensive studies on children's well-being, health equity, and women's economic security. David published several publications and books. He can be reached at wordsnum@optonline.net.

Since 1984, Words & Numbers Research, Inc. has conducted numerous evaluation and research studies in the fields of education, healthcare, manufacturing, banking, human services, and others. External evaluation services have been provided to the National Science Foundation and the US Department of Education. The firm conducts surveys, focus groups, and in-depth interviews. The office can be reached by phone at 860-489-5639, by email at wordsnum@optonline.net or on website at www.wordsandnumbersresearch.com.

www.ingramcontent.com/pod-product-compliance
Lightning Source LLC
Chambersburg PA
CBHW031712230426
43668CB00006B/193